Excel

BASIC SKILLS

COMPREHENSION AND WRITTEN EXPRESSION

YEAR 5

A. Horsfield

PASCAL PRESS

Copyright © 1998 Alan Horsfield
Reprinted 1999, 2001, 2002, 2004, 2005, 2006, 2007

ISBN 978 1 86441 280 2

Pascal Press
PO Box 250
Glebe NSW 2037
(02) 8585 4044
www.pascalpress.com.au

Text design and typesetting by Scriptorium Desktop Publishing Pty Ltd
Cover by Dizign
Printed by SNP Security Printing

Reproduction and communication for educational purposes

The Australian *Copyright Act 1968* (the Act) allows a maximum of one chapter or 10% of the pages of this work, whichever is the greater, to be reproduced and/or communicated by any educational institution for its educational purposes provided that the educational institution (or the body that administers it) has given a remuneration notice to Copyright Agency Limited (CAL) under the Act.

For details of the CAL licence for educational institutions contact:
Copyright Agency Limited
Level 19, 157 Liverpool Street
Sydney NSW 2000
Telephone: (02) 9394 7600
Facsimile: (02) 9394 7601
E-mail: info@copyright.com.au

Reproduction and communication for other purposes

Except as permitted under the Act (for example a fair dealing for the purposes of study, research, criticism or review) no part of this book may be reproduced, stored in a retrieval system, communicated or transmitted in any form or by any means without prior written permission. All inquiries should be made to the publisher at the address above.

Contents

	Page
To the parent and teacher	**iv**
Practice Comprehension Exercises	
Finding facts	1
Finding the main idea	7
Making inferences	13
Using context clues	17
Drawing conclusions	21
Noting detail	25
Following directions	29
Understanding questions	33
Understanding paragraphs	37
Relevant and irrelevant information	39
Fact and opinion	43
Understanding persuasion	47
Understanding and using tables of contents	51
Understanding and using an index	53
Using timetables	55
Understanding maps	57
Understanding graphs and charts	59
Answers	**Lift-out section**

Acknowledgements

Elaine Horsfield of EJH Talent Promotion P/L for support, typing and proof reading, Ian Rohr (Pascal Press) for his pertinent comments and those students who gave up their free time to 'test' the test writer.

The Big Race by A. Horsfield, buzzwords, International Thomas Publishing, Australia 1997

The Lemming Run by A. Horsfield from Then & Now, Wannabee Publishing 1977

To the parent and teacher

When the student completes the exercises in this book she/he will have worked through a number of question types from a variety of text types.

Rather than give a range of question types based on each passage, the focus in this book will be on developing the student's skill with a particular question type. The book is structured so that if there is a weakness or a 'gap' then the student can concentrate on that and become competent without working through passages that may not contribute to the student's progress.

With the help of an adult, the student will be able to focus on those skills that are appropriate.

Each new section provides information on what is required for the particular skill being practised. The first extract in each section is intended to lead the student through a number of questions based upon a specific skill. Brief answers and guidelines for finding answers are provided at the end of the exercise. A full set of answers is provided in the middle of the book.

This book uses a range of text types so that the student will feel confident in a variety of situations. Text types are usually broken into two broad categories; literary and factual. Within each group are numerous varieties — some are listed below. All texts, except for the two timetables, the mobile phone ad' and one small extract, are taken from the Spectrum Blue series or the associated teachers' resource books. The title of the book used is given at the start of each section. This allows the student to follow up exercises with recreational reading or reading for a specific purpose.

Literary texts include narratives (novels/stories), poetry and (drama) scripts.

Factual texts include explanations, expositions, information reports, recounts and procedures.

As you can see the list is quite long. It is important that students develop comprehension skills from a variety of text types. Many types of writing overlap.

On a number of occasions extracts are reused. This is done to demonstrate that different comprehension skills can be developed from the same piece of writing. Comprehension skills are interdependent.

Questions types include those that require:

- true–false responses
- multiple choice responses
- short answer responses
- full sentence answers
- matching exercises
- sentence completing
- sequencing
- open ended responses.

It is suggested that students should give full sentence answers unless directed otherwise. Sufficient space is allowed for such answers.

Good luck,

Alan Horsfield
T. Cert, BA, B Ed, M Ed, TESL Cert,
Dip Sch Admin

Finding Facts **1**

Finding Facts — Introduction

When finding facts you will often be asked questions beginning with Who, When, Where, What and How, and sometimes Why. You will be asked to search for answers to questions that help you understand the **time (when)** and **place (where)** of the action in the extract, as well as **who** or **what** is involved. **Which** may also be used. Sometimes you will be asked to give **names** or make **lists**. In this extract the words in brackets will help you find the facts.

You will be asked to search for answers to questions that help you understand either factual material or narratives (stories).

Most exercises in this part of the book are based upon factual writing. The story, *Paddock for a Pony* is an example of **realistic writing** so it is a good book to start 'finding facts'. You should answer with full sentence answers unless told to do otherwise. Full sentence answers help you to think through the answer you are going to give.

Now read the extract from *Paddock for a Pony* by Elizabeth Best.

<u>What</u> had actually happened was this. (*This sentence tells you that you are going to be given some facts.*)

Deborah, Pat and Billy (*Who*) had been playing in the paddock, finishing off a tree-house made of palings, high in the largest Moreton Bay Fig.

There were some other children also in the paddock, playing over near the shrubs beside Mr Crunkhorn's house.

Pat, Deborah and Billy had been so absorbed in their task they had been only vaguely aware of the yapping of the silkies until Mr Crunkhorn's bellowing made them pay attention. As they looked up they saw the other children, under the cover of the shrubs, slip quietly away (*what*).

A moment later Mr Crunkhorn's angry face appeared above the fence and between the shrubs. (*when*)

He saw Billy, Deborah and Pat in the middle of the paddock and thought it had been them tormenting the dogs.

He shook his stick at them (*how* — he threatened), threatened to tell their parents and ordered them out of the paddock. (*what he did*) Then he disappeared again behind the fence. (*where*)

The children were infuriated. (*who, and how/why they reacted*)

---

1. **Who** was building the tree house? **Suggested answer.** Deborah, Pat and Billy were building the tree house.

2. **What** did Pat, Deborah and Billy see when they looked up? *Pat, Deborah and Billy saw other children in the shrubs (looked up).*

3. **How** did Mr Crunkhorn threaten the children? *He shook his stick at them.*

4. Tick the best ending for this sentence. After leaving the children Mr Crunkhorn went

   ☐ under the fig tree. ☑ behind the fence. ☐ to the middle of the paddock.

Answers
1. Deborah, Pat and Billy were building the tree-house, 2. Pat, Deborah and Billy saw the other children when they looked up, 3. Mr Crunkhorn threatened the children with a stick/threatened to tell their parents, 4. behind the fence

Finding Facts — Strange Mysteries

by Rachael Collinson

The Boy Who Could Bend Spoons

Uri Geller was different from other little boys.

At the age of three, he surprised his mother by bending her spoons and soup ladles just by staring at them.

His grandmother's watch stopped, and Uri started it going again simply by rubbing the glass with his finger.

By the early 1970s, Uri Geller was famous in his own country, Israel, and throughout the world, for his amazing performances. He would bend spoons, read minds, start broken watches and clocks, and draw pictures which exactly matched those drawn by somebody in another room.

Whenever he appeared on stage, on the radio and on television, people would notice strange things happening in the audience and around the house.

Their cutlery would bend all by itself, their broken clocks would start chiming and their car keys and house keys would bend so badly that they would be unable to get into their cars or open their front doors.

Eventually scientists suggested that Uri undergo a series of tests, so he was invited to Standford Research Institute in the USA, and given several feats to perform.

One test had Uri concentrating very hard on a magnetometer, which measures the strength of a magnetic field.

The scientists said 'although it was scientifically impossible', the needle moved each time Uri was asked to concentrate on it.

1. When did Uri first surprise his mother? _He bent his mothers spoons and scrip saddles by just staring at them._

2. What did Uri do that surprised his mother? _at the age of 3._

Answer **True** or **False** to these facts.

3. By 1970 Uri's fame had become worldwide. _true_

4. Uri could make watches start by rubbing the glass. _false_

5. Uri could break car keys. _false_

6. Uri first used his powers to entertain people. _true_

7. The scientists tested Uri's special powers by using a (circle one answer)

    door key   (magnet)   spoon   watch   clock

8. Circle the most important fact. (a) Uri appeared on stage   (b) car doors wouldn't open

    (c) Uri could draw pictures   (d) magnet needles moved   (e) (audiences were amazed)

Finding Facts — Tell Me How

by Mike Callaghan, Peter Knapp, Ross Latham and Peter Sloan

How do ants live?

Ants are social insects that live in large groups called colonies. There are more than 10 000 kinds of ants and they are more numerous than any other land animal. All ants in the colony have special jobs and social responsibilities. Colonies of ants live in well-organised places called nests.

There are three types of ants in a colony: a queen, the female workers and the male ants. The queen ant produces eggs which are cared for by the female worker ants. The male ants are only produced for mating. Most of the ants in a colony are female worker ants.

X _____

Male ants and new queen ants have wings and are produced in the summer months by the queen of an established colony. When the weather is warm enough they leave the nests for the wedding flight where they mate while flying. After they have mated the male ant falls to the ground and dies. The queen then flies down to the ground and soon after sheds her wings. Once on the ground the queen begins building a new nest.

Choose the best answer to complete questions 1 and 2.

1. In each colony of ants there are

☑ 10 000 kinds of ants.

☐ three types of ants.

☐ more males than females.

☐ many ants laying eggs.

2. Male ants start flying

☐ when their wings are fully formed.

☑ when it is time to build a new nest.

☐ before summer comes.

☐ after the new queen leaves the nest.

3. Writers use sub-headings to highlight main points or important facts. In this extract the writer has included a sub-heading at the point where there is the **X**.

A good title for the sub-heading would be

☒ How is a new colony started?

☐ Where do ants go?

☐ Which ants are the most important?

☐ When do male ants leave the nest?

4. The male dies after mating with the new queen. True ☑ False ☐

5. All ants in an ant colony have a special job. True ☑ False ☐

6. All female ants lay eggs. True ☐ False ☑

7. Complete this sentence. Most ants in an ant colony are _female works_ .

Finding Facts—The Portland Fairy Penguins

by Edel Wignell

Fairy penguins come ashore in several places around the harbour and foreshore of Portland Bay. Some are visitors from Phillip Island or other parts of the coast.

About one hundred fairy penguins nest in scattered colonies at Portland Bay.

Many penguins nest in artificial burrows, such as pipes. They find holes among loose and broken rocks along the harbour's breakwaters and banks, and among scrap metal and stacks of materials along the wharves.

The colonies vary in size: there may be only two burrows, or there may be twenty-five. Usually the Portland Bay penguins lay two eggs.

Only about 40 per cent of chicks reach one year of age. Most die of natural causes. Perhaps there is not enough food, and they starve. Perhaps they are killed by a disease caused by parasites. They might be eaten by a shark or a seal soon after they go to sea.

Wildlife officers and naturalists have been banding the Portland Bay penguins since 1979, and studying their habits. During that time huge silos, factories and wharves have been built along the foreshore.

Portland is a busy industrial city with 12 000 people. It was Victoria's first settlement — established one year before Melbourne was begun.

Choose the best answer to complete questions 1 and 2.

1. Many penguin chicks die
   - [ ] from pollution.
   - [ ] because of hunters.
   - [✓] of natural causes.
   - [ ] from attacks from feral animals.

2. Wildlife officers
   - [ ] save penguins from shark attacks.
   - [ ] protect penguins from disease.
   - [✓] have banded penguins for many years.
   - [ ] settled in Portland before going to Melbourne.

3. Which fact **CANNOT** be found in the extract?
   - [✓] Fairy penguins make good pets.
   - [ ] Fairy penguins can nest among building materials.
   - [ ] Fairy penguins are surviving in a shipping port.
   - [ ] Fairy penguins come ashore in several different places.

4. Fairy penguins lay one or two eggs each nesting season. True [✓] False [ ]

5. Fairy penguins will not nest in anything but a natural burrow. True [ ] False [✓]

6. In your opinion why would wildlife officers band and study penguins? _To find out how they live and increase their numbers._

Finding Facts — The Sylvia Mystery

by Penny Hall

Over the Fence

Kat stood at her open bedroom window and scowled down at the pool in its carefully landscaped setting, two storeys below. The water was the same brilliant, unlikely blue as the water in the toilet bowls — and just as irritating in its synthetic perfection. She drank a last swig of Coke, burped loudly and tossed the can into the pool.

No adult voice bellowed in disapproval; no child's voice giggled in appreciation.

The can bobbed on the gentle waves generated by the automatic pool cleaner, slid gradually into the water and finally sank.

It's not fair, Kat moaned inwardly. It's going to be another stinking hot day. For the first time in my life I've got a pool in the backyard, and I'm not allowed to use it till they come home.

For five whole days, the yard, enclosed by its high brush fence, had been like a park for her private use.

Exploring the house and its electronic gadgets had been fun. Now, her park was beginning to feel like a gaol and there was only so much she could do on her own in a strange house.

She could see little slices of the neighbouring houses but trees blocked out most of her view.

Privacy! she thought disgustedly. If that's what they pay all those thousands of dollars for here, they can keep it!

1. How many people are with Kat? (short answer) _No one._

2. Kat tossed her drink can

- [ ] into the scrap bin.
- [✓] into the pool.
- [ ] onto the floor.
- [ ] over the fence.

3. Kat felt her new home was like a

- [ ] holiday resort.
- [ ] park.
- [ ] backyard.
- [✓] gaol.

4. Circle the word that best describes Kat's feeling after being in the house for a week.

excited   thrilled   worried   (bored)   satisfied

5. Kat was only allowed to use the pool in the morning.   True [ ]   False [✓]

6. Kat thought privacy was to be treasured.   True [ ]   False [✓]

7. What information (fact) tells you that the residents kept to themselves?

_____

6 Excel Comprehension Skillbuilder Year 5

Finding Facts — What a Waste!

by Stephen Jones

Recycling

Recycling is not a new way of dealing with waste. Old clothes and rags have been recycled for a long time. So have papers, bottles and scrap metal. The cry of the bottle collector, 'Bottles. Bottle-O' used to be heard regularly in our streets. Until the 1960s, most people paid a deposit when they bought a bottle of drink and got their money back when they returned the bottle. However, as more and more of our containers became non-returnable and more and more of our products were made to be thrown away, less and less of our waste was recycled.

Now people are starting to realise the problems caused by so much waste. Recycling is increasing. When we recycle waste, we treat it so that new products can be made from it. Most local councils now collect paper and cardboard, glass and some plastic bottles for recycling and in some areas, steel cans are collected. Aluminium cans are already collected by service clubs, schools, sports teams and charities. At home, we can recycle food scraps and garden waste as compost.

Even though 70%–80 % of our household rubbish can be recycled, our recycling system is not very good. The problem seems to be that:

- many people do not put waste out for councils to collect for recycling.
- not many products that people want to buy are available in recycled material. This is particularly so with plastics.
- many waste products are not easy to recycle.

1. Draw a line from the sentence beginnings to an ending to make the facts correct.

Most household rubbish — a new way of dealing with rubbish.

Recycling is — can be recycled.

When we recycle waste — we use it to make new products.

2. What is this extract about? The extract _is about Recycling._

3. In the 1960s there was a charge on drink bottles. This was called a _Deposit._

4. These days there are fewer throw-away containers. True ☐ False ✓

5. People are still trying to find a way to recycle household rubbish. True ✓ False ✓ ⊗

6. Write one fact you learnt from the extract. _Recycling is good for the inviroment._

7. Tick the best ending for this sentence.
According to the extract, most of the failure of the recycling program can be blamed on

☐ local councils.

☐ manufacturers of plastic.

✓ ordinary householders.

☐ service clubs and charities.

Finding the Main Idea — Introduction

When reading paragraphs you will often be asked to find the **main idea**. The main idea is often the same as the **topic sentence**. It is the most important piece of information for the reader. All other sentences in the paragraph add to the meaning of the topic sentence. They are often called the **supporting detail**. **Bullet points** (•) are often used to list important supporting detail.

The topic sentence is often the first sentence but it can come in the middle of the paragraph or at the end. The topic sentence, if it is quite long, may sometimes contain more information than just the main idea.

Paragraphs are usually made up of more than one sentence (see Understanding Paragraphs, p. 37). Titles and headings often give the main idea in books or in chapters. If we look at the extract, *What a Waste*, again we can use it to start 'finding the main idea'. Any piece of writing can be used for more than one type of comprehension question.

What a Waste!

by Stephen Jones

Recycling

Recycling is not a new way of dealing with waste. (*main idea/topic sentence*) Old clothes and rags have been recycled for a long time. (*supporting detail*) So have papers, bottles and scrap metal. The cry of the bottle collector, 'Bottles. Bottle-O' used to be heard regularly in our streets. Until the 1960s, most people paid a deposit when they bought a bottle of drink and got their money back when they returned the bottle. However, as more and more of our containers became non-returnable and more and more of our products were made to be thrown away, less and less of our waste was recycled.

Now people are starting to realise the problems caused by so much waste. Recycling is increasing. When we recycle waste, we treat it so that new products can be made from it. Most local councils now collect paper and cardboard, glass and some plastic bottles for recycling and in some areas, steel cans are collected. Aluminium cans are already collected by service clubs, schools, sports teams and charities. At home, we can recycle food scraps and garden waste as compost.

Even though 70%–80 % of our household rubbish can be recycled, our recycling system is not very good. (*main idea*) The problem seems to be that:

- many people do not put waste out for councils to collect for recycling. (*supporting detail*)
- not many products that people want to buy are available in recycled material. This is particularly so with plastics. (*supporting detail*)
- many waste products are not easy to recycle. (*supporting detail*)

1. How many paragraphs in this extract? _____ 3

2. How many topic sentences would you expect to find? _____ 3

3. In the last paragraph, how many points are listed as **bullet points**? _____ 3

4. Which of the following could be a good heading for this extract? (circle one)

   Old Clothes   Councils Help with Waste   (The Problem of Waste)

5. From paragraph 2, write out the sentence you think carries the main idea.

   Recycling is not a new way of dealing with waste.

6. Paragraph 1 has support information about the recycling of bottles.   True ✓   False ☐

Answers 1. three, 2. three, 3. three, 4. The Problem of Waste is the best heading. The other options are about details. 5. Recycling is increasing. 6. True

8 Excel Comprehension Skillbuilder Year 5

Finding the Main Idea — Time Capsule

by Rachael Collinson

To help you the paragraphs have been numbered in this extract.

1. This is a story about time. It starts about a hundred years ago …
2. It was the start of a strange day for Anne Woodhouse and her brother, James.
3. The sun shone through the window onto Anne's face. She blinked.
4. The sound of the horses, snorting and stamping outside, soon had her wide awake. The clock in the hall chimed the hour of eight.
5. Anne sat up in bed. Although the day was already warm, a shiver ran through her body.
6. What was it that made her feel so strange? Was it a dream? She sensed some strange object, some mysterious shape at the edge of her mind. How odd, she thought. It seemed almost there, then suddenly disappeared.
7. Cousin Elizabeth had something to do with it. But Anne did not know what.
8. Anne pushed back the covers and stepped onto the wooden floor. She walked slowly over to the window.
9. Everything seemed normal. The familiar land stretched out before her. The sun caught the flutter of birds and the gentle swaying of eucalyptus trees. There were Mother and Father, walking by the fence.

1. Which paragraph starts with a question sentence? paragraph _6_

2. Write the topic sentence for the first paragraph. _This is a story about time._

3. Which sentence is the main idea of the last paragraph? (tick one box)

- [✓] Everything seemed normal.
- [ ] The familiar land stretched out before her.
- [ ] The sun caught the flutter of birds and the gentle swaying of eucalyptus trees.
- [ ] There were Mother and Father, walking by the fence.

4. Using your own words, how would you describe what is happening in paragraph 6?
Ann has a weird feeling.

5. Select the best title for this extract. (tick one box)

- [ ] A Horse Story
- [✓] Strange Feelings
- [ ] Happy Days
- [ ] Life in the Country

6. Anne woke up feeling worried about her parents. True [ ] False [✓]

7. Anne's strange feeling stayed with her all morning. True [ ] False [✓]

Finding the Main Idea — Battlers of the Great Depression

by Edel Wignell

The Great Depression

The Great Depression of the 1930s was a worldwide financial disaster. It all began in the United States, with the Wall Street Crash of 1929.

America was prosperous in the 1920s. People invested in the stock market, and many made a fortune. They borrowed money from the banks on the strength of their shares. The more shares were sold, the more prices fell. Investors began to panic and tried to sell their shares before they became worthless. Prices fell even further and finally the stock market collapsed. People couldn't repay their bank loans because their stocks and shares were worthless. They went broke, and so did the banks.

The crash destroyed the American economy and soon the effects were felt throughout the world.

Factories and businesses closed down or dismissed many workers. Millions of people could not find work, and many families were hungry.

The worst years of the Depression were 1929–34, but for many people, life was difficult for ten years or more afterwards. The Second World War (1939–45) was a time of hunger, too. So the years 1929–50 were a time of hunger and poverty for millions of people around the world.

1. How many paragraphs in this extract? _5_

2. What is the topic sentence for the second paragraph? _America was prosperous in 1920's_

3. The second last paragraph (starts with 'Factories …') tells why people were hungry.

   People had no money because _People had no money because they couldn't find work._

4. According to the extract life was difficult

   ☐ for the period of the Great Depression only.   ☐ during the 1920s.

   ☐ for the time of the Second World War only.   ☑ for the period 1929 to 1950.

5. What major event followed the Great Depression? (short answer) _2nd world war. second world war._

6. If you had to give the extract a title, a good one would be

   ☐ American Prosperity.   ☐ Worthless Money.

   ☐ Banks go Broke.   ☑ Years of Difficulty.

7. The third paragraph is very short. What important idea does it tell the reader? _The disaster had an effect worldwide._

8. The second paragraph explains how you should do your banking.   True ☐   False ☑

Finding the Main Idea — Made For Australia

by Judith Kendra

Solar Energy

The sun's energy is very useful. It will never run out and it is also free. In some ways Australia is lucky because it receives more of the sun's rays than almost any other country in the world. Therefore, as the costs of fuels like oil and gas rise, it makes sense to use the sun's rays as much as possible. Now we use solar energy to heat our homes, provide hot water, and to drive pumps and other things.

Solar heating works by putting collectors, which are sometimes called solar cells, on the roof or walls of a house. These collectors catch the sun and convert its energy into heat. In the remote parts of Australia electricity can cost far more than it does in the cities. About 6 per cent of Australian homes have solar water heaters at the moment, but this number is rising.

The biggest factory in the world for making solar water heaters is in Western Australia. Recently a highly efficient silicon solar cell was developed at the University of New South Wales. Also, in 1977, scientists at the Australian National University in Canberra made the world's first system for storing large amounts of solar energy.

1. Which paragraph tells the reader about the importance of solar power? Para. _____

2. Draw a line to match the main idea in the paragraph with the paragraph number.

Paragraph 1   development of solar power cells

Paragraph 2   importance of solar power for Australia

Paragraph 3   how solar heating works

3. If you had to give the extract a title, a good one would be

☐ Western Australian Factories.   ☑ Power for the Future.

☐ University Scientists.   ☐ The Sun Always Shines.

4. Which paragraph tells the reader about scientific research in Australia?

☐ Paragraph 1   ☐ Paragraph 2   ☑ Paragraph 3

5. Which idea is NOT included in the extract on solar power?

(A) supplying solar power to factories   (C) storing solar energy

(B) water heating and solar power   (D) the cost of solar energy

6. Paragraph three is mainly about the size of factories.   True ☐   False ☑

7. According to the extract the cost of oil and gas will rise.   True ☑   False ☐

8. Complete this sentence. Electricity costs more in the ___country___ than the city.

Finding the Main Idea — Saving Wildlife

by Edel Wignell

Decoy gannets

In January 1988 there were six gannets (sea birds) on Cat Island, an islet east of Flinders Island in Bass Strait. Eighty years ago a huge colony of 10 000 gannets nested there. In 1950 there were only 200 left. The numbers decreased until, in 1984, a bush-fire killed most of the remaining few birds.

Humans were the gannets' main enemies. Some fishermen killed them to use as bait in crayfish pots. Other people used them as targets for shooting.

The Australasian gannet is a large bird with a white and black body and golden feathers on its head. In flight its wings stretch almost two metres across.

For ten years, officers of the Department of Lands, Parks and Wildlife had been trying to get gannets to come back to their old breeding ground. In 1987 and 1988 fake gannets were used as decoys.

The decoy gannets were moulded from polyurethane and wire, and weighted with bricks. They were painted by school children on Flinders Island, who took care with all the details, such as eye and beak markings.

The decoys were very lifelike. From a distance it is difficult to tell which is a fake and which is a real bird. When the fake birds were put on Cat Island in 1987, gannets landed immediately. They started tapping beaks with the decoys.

In that first year, one started nesting among the decoys. In 1988 six gannets arrived, nested, and hatched three chicks.

Other birds have been fooled by the decoys. A pair of sea eagles (enemies of the gannets) swooped and attacked. They damaged some of the decoys by ripping at them with their talons, tearing their heads off and smashing their beaks.

Everyone, including the children who painted the decoys, hopes that the gannets have returned permanently, and that their numbers will rise every year.

1. How many paragraphs in this extract? __*9*__

2. Here is the sixth paragraph. Tick the box to show which is the main idea (topic sentence).

   [✓] The decoys were very lifelike.

   [ ] From a distance it is difficult to tell which is a fake and which is a real bird.

   [ ] When the fake birds were put on Cat Island in 1987, gannets landed immediately.

   [ ] They started tapping beaks with the decoys.

3. If you had to give the extract another title, a good one would be

   [✓] Saving the Gannets.   [ ] Eagle Attack.

   [ ] Making Model Gannets.   [ ] Vandalism.

4. The first time decoys were put on the island one gannet nested there. True [✓] False [ ]

5. The problem with the decoys was that they didn't fool animals.   True [ ] False [✓]

6. The extract is mainly concerned with *Encouraging to return to their nesting grounds.*

7. Circle the correct word in the brackets. People were concerned that gannets would die out on ((Cat)   Flinders) Island.

Finding the Main Idea — My Neighbours at Nagin

by Judy Parker

Kashmir is a region in the far north of India, near the snow-capped Himalayan mountains. Srinagar, the capital of the city, is famous for its houseboats, moored in colourful rows on the lakes of Dal and Nagin. About a hundred years ago, when Great Britain ruled most of India, Kashmir was a popular summer retreat for those wishing to escape the extreme heat of the Indian plains. The Maharaja, the ruler of Kashmir, would not let the British people buy any land in Kashmir, so they cleverly decided to build ornate houseboats and live on the lakes instead.

The houseboats are beautifully hand-carved out of deodar pine. The furniture is also hand-carved, and its dark walnut wood is polished to a brilliant sheen. Shining brass vases and papier mache lamps decorate the tables. The wooden floors are covered with brightly coloured, hand-woven carpets. Steep stairs lead up to the sun deck from the entrance galley. Most houseboats have three large bedrooms and a dining room with a grand table and heavy, carved chairs.

Moored to the back of the houseboats and beached in the shallow canals at the lake's shore are the doongas. Doongas are flat, plain houseboats where Kashmiri houseboat owners live. It is on the doongas that the food is cooked for the overseas travellers staying on the houseboats.

1. Using your own words, write what paragraph 1 is about (main idea). _____
The origins of Kashmiri ~~h~~ houseboats in Kashmir

2. The second paragraph is mainly about (tick one box)

☐ the wood used in houseboats.   ☐ keeping houseboats clean.

☐ the interior (inside) of a houseboat.   ☐ carving houseboat furniture.

3. The last paragraph is mainly about

☑ where houseboat owners live.   ☐ the difference between houseboats and doongas.

☐ cleaning houseboats.   ☐ looking after international travellers.

4. The information about Britain ruling India is supporting detail.   True ☑   False ☐

5. Doongas are found in canals.   True ☑   False ☐

6. Houseboats are much smaller than doongas.   True ☐   False ☑

7. Write the topic sentence for the last paragraph.(be careful) _Doongas are_
flat, plain house boats where khashmiri houseboat

8. The British began to build ornate houseboats because they couldn't buy land on which to _own_
build their homes. This information is: ☑ supporting detail   ☐ the main idea   _live_

9. Which timber is not used in the buiding of houseboats?   deodar   <u>cedar</u>   walnut

Making Inferences **13**

Making Inferences — Introduction

Making an inference is a thinking or reasoning skill (see also Drawing Conclusions p. 21). The reader is often only given a limited amount of information. The reader makes inferences from the information given. Readers also use their general knowledge when making inferences.

> Let's read this small passage.
> Claude McGhee was in Year Six.
> He was the biggest kid in school,
> and he hadn't got his nickname,
> Claws, for nothing. He was built
> like a bear but he could also run.
>
> from *The Big Race*, A. Horsfield

The reader could make several inferences from this passage. What sort of a person is Claude McGhee? How did he *really* get his nickname? From the evidence, the reader could probably **infer** that Claws was a bully, or someone to be frightened of.

Sometimes writers will deliberately mislead the reader. They do not give all the information or they add information that gives the reader the wrong ideas or impressions. This happens in mystery stories and some scary (horror) books.

Read the extract from *The Sylvia Mystery* by Penny Hall.

Over the Fence

Kat stood at her open bedroom window and scowled down at the pool in its carefully landscaped setting, two storeys below. The water was the same brilliant, unlikely blue as the water in the toilet bowls — and just as irritating in its synthetic perfection. She drank a last swig of Coke, burped loudly and tossed the can into the pool.

No adult voice bellowed in disapproval; no child's voice giggled in appreciation.

The can bobbed on the gentle waves generated by the automatic pool cleaner, slid gradually into the water and finally sank.

It's not fair, Kat moaned inwardly. It's going to be another stinking hot day. For the first time in my life I've got a pool in the backyard, and I'm not allowed to use it till they come home.

For five whole days, the yard, enclosed by its high brush fence, had been like a park for her private use.

Exploring the huge house with its electronic gadgets had been fun. Now her park was beginning to feel like a gaol and there was only so much she could do, on her own, in a strange house.

She could see little slices of the neighbouring houses but trees blocked out most of her view.

---

1. The reader could infer that Kat was alone in the building. What information makes the reader think this? **Suggested answer.** No adult voice bellowed in disapproval when she tossed her can into the pool. (Other answers are possible.)

2. What information has Penny Hall given to infer that Kat is not really a naughty person?

---

3. Kat's new house is quite modern. This can be inferred from the fact that (tick one box)

☐ it is a huge house with many electronic gadgets   ☐ trees block most of the view

Short answers   1. This one has been done for you. 2. Kat wouldn't go into the pool without permission. 3. huge house with electronic gadgets

Making Inferences — The Incredible Experience of Megan Kingsley

by Pamela O'Connor

She was bound hand and foot, unable to move, being stoned to death.

She couldn't see where the rocks were coming from. They just came from nowhere, mostly hitting her legs. A stray stone landed on her arm. She tried to scream, but no sound would come out.

At last they stopped and she thought her tormentors had gone away. But no! They were going to drown her instead!

Megan woke, spluttering and shivering as the cold water ran over her face and down her neck and back.

Patrick rolled over laughing hysterically as she sat up, wiping the water out of her eyes.

'Patrick Kingsley, I hate you!' she screamed. 'Why do you always have to be so revolting!'

'You wouldn't wake up.' Patrick squatted a safe distance away, still chuckling. 'And I thought you might be dead so I threw some pebbles on your legs. When that didn't work, I thought the cold water might do the trick.'

'Where is Aurora?' Megan felt stiff and cold.

'Dunno.' replied Patrick. 'Were you out there all night?' He laid some sticks and got a fire going.

'I must have been. Last thing I remember I was lying here talking to Aurora.'

And then she had a dream. Didn't she? It had seemed so real.

---

1. The writer, Pamela O' Connor, wants the reader to think something dreadful is happening to Megan. What is really happening? Megan _____.

2. Patrick is lighting a fire. From this, you could infer that (Tick as many boxes as you need.)

- ☐ The night had been cold.
- ☐ Patrick and Megan are on holidays.
- ☐ Patrick is about to cook breakfast.
- ☐ Megan needs to dry off after getting wet.

3. Megan's dream seems very realistic because Patrick was

- ☐ throwing stones at her.
- ☐ screaming at her.
- ☐ being revolting.
- ☐ chuckling to himself.

4. Once she had woken up, Megan was sure she had been dreaming. True ☐ False ☐

5. Patrick and Megan had been awake since Aurora had left. True ☐ False ☐

Making Inferences — The Secret of Yesterday Hills

by Elsie Young

There had been nightly arguments between his parents for the last few weeks. Well, who would want to leave the beaut Gold Coast? He'd always lived there. It had amusement arcades and Seaworld and Dreamworld and the beaches of course. The surf carnivals were OK too, and there was TV. There was only one channel where they were going. It was rotten luck all right, his father being transferred by the bank. 'Promoted' to manager in this horrible little town with the silly name, Mullawalla.

Frank tore open another bag of salted peanuts. A frown had been parked on his face since they'd left the coast two days before. 'I'm tired,' he whined, but really he felt ill. The two meat pies he'd insisted he could eat for lunch hadn't settled too happily with all the cold drinks, and the fruit slice with cream seemed to be pressing heavily on top. No answer from in front. Fat lot they cared! They didn't have to go to a rotten new school with a lot of dumb bush kids.

The car's fast motion was making his head dizzy and his stomach lurched uneasily. He was thirsty again. He finished the warm dregs of his orange drink. All the windows were closed for the air-conditioning but the red dust still seeped in and irritated his nose and eyes. He closed his eyes and almost dozed. It was no good.

'Ooooh!' he screamed. 'Stop! I'm going to be sick!'

1. From the extract you can infer that Frank (Tick as many boxes as you need.)

☐ didn't like TV all that much.

☐ enjoyed where he had been living.

☐ was going on holidays.

☐ was pleased about his father's promotion.

2. What do you think Frank's parents argued about? (Tick one box.)

☐ the cost of buying a new house.

☐ living in a small country town.

☐ Frank getting car sick.

☐ finding a school for Frank.

3. Frank's sickness was caused by eating too many peanuts.　True ☐　False ☐

4. Everyone was enjoying the trip out into the country.　True ☐　False ☐

5. Why do you think Frank pretended to feel tired? (Give your reason.) _____

_____

6. Frank could best be described as feeling

☐ anxious.　　☐ uncooperative.　　☐ excited.　　☐ disinterested.

7. Which one of the following finally made Frank sick?

(A) his parent's arguments　　(B) the orange drink　　(C) the red dust

Making Inferences — Own Up!

by Ellen Robertson

Mrs Lovejoy was all smiles when she walked into the Year 5 classroom. The children smiled back nervously. They were waiting for Mrs Lovejoy to 'discover' the new Mrs McSnorty.

As Mrs Lovejoy walked to the back of the classroom, the heads all turned at the same time.

'Why, Mrs McSnorty, what's happened? Nodded off, have you? Never mind, we'll wake you up, dear.' When Mrs Lovejoy shook the 'new' Mrs McSnorty, the head fell off!

Mrs Lovejoy put one hand on her hip and the other to her forehead. Looking around the classroom, she seemed terribly anxious.

'We can explain,' said Richard. 'It was an accident.'

'What do you mean, Richard? Where is the real Mrs McSnorty? I do hope she's all right. You could all be in a great deal of trouble, you know.'

'We know,' they chorused.

'Well, then, tell me what happened.'

Taking it in turns, they recounted their adventure for Mrs Lovejoy. Her eyebrows kept going up and down. After a while, she stared out the window and didn't seem to be listening at all. But she was.

1. From the extract you can infer that Mrs McSnorty (Tick as many boxes as you need.)

☐ is in the staffroom having lunch.

☐ has been involved in a strange incident.

☐ is marking books in the back of the room.

☐ was hurt in a dreadful accident.

2. Mrs Lovejoy was concerned about her class because (Tick one box.)

☐ Mrs McSnorty had gone to sleep in the classroom.

☐ the class was being very well behaved.

☐ the children didn't warn her about Mrs McSnorty's head.

☐ something was happening she didn't understand.

3. All the children knew about Mrs McSnorty.   True ☐   False ☐

4. Mrs Lovejoy thought the children were lying.   True ☐   False ☐

5. Why do you think the children were nervous? (Give your reason.) _____

_____

6. While listening to the children, Mrs Lovejoy could be described as being

☐ thoughtful.   ☐ nervous.   ☐ disinterested.   ☐ annoyed.

Using Context Clues — Introduction

Sometimes, when we read, we are not always told all the information directly. Often we can work out the meaning of a sentence or word by looking at the sentences around it. The context can also give clues to the meaning of new or unusual words.

Read this short passage.

The bodies were packed together on the street, waiting. The crowd wasn't unruly. It was quiet, subdued, fending off the winter chill by sheer bulk of numbers. Like penguins guarding their eggs during a winter blizzard. Forever slowly swirling, never wanting to be exposed to the elements, to the dangers of being left exposed and vulnerable on the outer ring of the masses. Men and women, but mostly men, talking to one another in secretive tones.

The Lemming Run, A. Horsfield

From the text we get clues about what might be going on: something sinister seems about to happen (many people waiting in the cold). They seem frightened (no one wants to be on the edge of the crowd). We get this information from the **context** in which it appears. We use **context clues**.

Read this extract from *Going Fishing With My Dad* by Jan Weeks

Note: The person who tells the story /poem is often called the narrator if we don't know his/her name.

'Fishing is the greatest fun,' said my father. Mum had asked him to mow the back lawn, but the mower wouldn't start so he was leaning over the back fence talking to our neighbours instead. They'd spent the weekend fishing and had come back with stacks of fish. We even had some in our refrigerator.

I thought fishing would be the greatest fun as well, so I jumped up and down and begged Dad to take me. Asking for something in front of neighbours was always a good idea. No father wanted to look mean in front of his neighbours. 'Sure, son,' he answered, patting my head.

'When?' I asked, trying to pin him to a definite date. All he said was 'One of these days,' which probably meant never.

During the next week I weeded the garden and pestered Dad to take me fishing. I washed the car and pestered Dad to take me fishing. I tidied the garage and pestered Dad to take me fishing.

'All right,' he said at last, worn down by my **persistence**.

---

1. What did the narrator like the best? (tick one box)

☐ cleaning the car   ☐ mowing the lawn

☐ going fishing   ☐ pestering his father

2. How often do you think the father and son went fishing? (give your reason) _____

_____

3. The word **persistence** could be replaced by (efforts   pestering). (circle one word)

4. The father was keen to get the lawn mowed.   True ☐   False ☐

Short answers   1. going fishing, 2. not often because the son hadn't gone on the last trip, (OR he had to pester his father to take him), 3. pestering, 4. False

Using Context Clues — Not Zackly

by Mary Small

Leigh and Julie were fed up with the weather, and so was Bandit. For the first **precious** week of the school holidays it had rained without stopping. There was water everywhere … pouring from the cloud-filled sky, running in rivulets down the face of the windowpanes, lying in muddy pools in the garden, cascading along the gutters in the street outside. There had been nothing else to do except stay dry indoors, reading and watching television.

Julie sat slumped in the beanbag, bored with the book she was reading. She looked up in surprise as a sudden shaft of sunlight beamed through the window.

'I don't believe it!' she said, scrambling to her feet. 'Leigh! It's stopped raining. There's blue sky outside. Enough to make a sailor a pair of trousers.'

Leigh, who had been trying to fix the propeller on to his model aeroplane, came up beside her. 'Let's get out and go for a walk,' he said, 'before it starts raining all over again.'

Walk? Bandit leaped to his feet. With a joyful yelp he rushed to the door and waited anxiously for it to be opened.

'We'd better tell Mum where we are going,' said Julie. 'Mum!' she shouted back into the house. 'we're going to the paddock to look at the creek.'

'Be careful,' called Jean.

1. Bandit is most likely

☐ Leigh's friend ☐ a cat ☐ Julie's sister ☐ a dog

2. The first week of the holidays is called precious because

☐ the children had only limited time to enjoy themselves.

☐ holidays are always very expensive.

☐ the children had little opportunity to spend their money.

☐ having a holiday is a rare event.

3. Jean probably told the children to be careful because she thought

☐ they might not get back before night. ☐ the creek might be in flood.

☐ it might start raining again. ☐ Bandit could catch a cold.

4. What was Julie doing when she shouted back into the house? _____

_____

5. What did Bandit do that would make you think he understood what people were

talking about? _____

6. When Julie said there was enough blue sky to make a sailor a pair of trousers she meant that the sky (**was completely blue**   **had blue patches**). (circle one answer)

Using Context Clues — Show Off

by Hazel Edwards

'Grade 5. Put your show entries on the side table, please.' Mrs Black pointed to the long table, already piled with plates of cakes, monster masks and rainbow-coloured knitting squares. My lop-sided purple pottery mug was there too.

Mrs Black believed that all her children should enter something in the show.

'Make sure your name and the section you want to enter is on the entry form,' she said, fumbling for extra pens. Since losing her glasses on Monday, Mrs Black couldn't see too well. Students chatted excitedly as they filled in the forms.

In last year's Grade 5, Amanda Browne won the prize for the 'Most imaginative creature' in the Art and Craft section. Her entry was a pineapple stuck with toothpicks to look like an echidna.

Mrs Black kept mentioning that. 'Perhaps this year's Grade 5 will win something too' — she must have said it ten times a day in the week before the show. 'Especially since we have Amanda's cousin in our class this year.'

Matthew Browne just kept staring at the spider crawling on the window sill.

Amanda was known for the things she did well. People always remembered Matthew for his mistakes. They remembered when Matthew spilt glue on the gym floor; got stuck in the roof when collecting tennis balls; or fell off the ladder into the Grade 2 herb garden. And they always remembered whose cousin he was.

1. Give two examples that suggest to the reader that Matthew was clumsy.

a) _____   b) _____

2. Which of the following sentences suggests that Matthew wasn't happy with his reputation?

- [ ] He was compared unfavourably with Amanda.
- [ ] He had made something to put in the show.
- [ ] He spilt glue on the floor of the gym.
- [ ] He watched a spider crawling up the wall.

3. Matthew's interest is more on the _____ than his show entry.

4. The children in Grade 5 thought that making an entry for the show had been (**hard work   good fun   too difficult   very costly**). (circle one answer)

5. From information in the extract it is most likely that Matthew will

- [ ] fill in his entry form correctly.
- [ ] cause some sort of disaster to happen.
- [ ] have a great entry for the show.
- [ ] be helped by Amanda.

6. Mrs Black expected Amanda's cousin to do well in the show.   True [ ]   False [ ]

7. This was the first time Mrs Black had talked about the show.   True [ ]   False [ ]

Using Context Clues — That Proverbial Cat

by Elizabeth Best

Curiosity, goes the saying, killed the cat.

'I wonder,' thought Darin, 'If curiosity could kill ours.'

He looked at Tiger, his own beloved puss, lying **placidly** on the carpet, half asleep, and to all outward appearances, most incurious. But appearances aren't everything.

'I simply must find out,' Darin thought. 'And if he is curious, I'll have to protect him in some way. I wouldn't like Tiger to get killed.'

So Darin lay down on the carpet a little distance away from Tiger and, like a true expert in these matters, he pretended to be asleep, while at the same time he watched the cat closely.

He did not want Tiger to become suspicious and **consequently** not act his own true self.

He did not have long to wait. Tiger eyed Darin sleepily for a few moments and then (in true cat **form**), his curiosity getting the better of him, he stood up, arching his back in a beautiful stretch.

'Aha!' thought Darin. 'He's moving.'

But to his great disgust, in another moment, he realised the cat's curiosity was only aroused by seeing his master lying on the carpet with his eyes shut and, once having investigated this occurrence, the animal curled up again in the curve between Darin's knees and stomach and went back to sleep.

1. The cat woke up because

- [ ] Darin made a lot of noise.
- [ ] it became curious about Darin.
- [ ] it needed to arch its back.
- [ ] Darin made it a new sleeping place.

2. The cat's reaction to Darin lying on the floor was (expected   unexpected). (circle one word)

3. The word 'form' could best be replaced with

- [ ] style.
- [ ] shape.
- [ ] belief
- [ ] control.

4. The word '**consequently**' could be replaced with (as a result   later   expectedly). (circle one)

5. Darin's method of finding out if curiosity kills cats is likely to fail. True [ ] False [ ]

6. If the cat was lying '**placidly**' it was lying **peacefully**.   True [ ] False [ ]

7. List two things Darin did that, he thought, made him seem like an expert.

a) _____   b)_____

8. When people say 'curiosity killed the cat' they mean people should not

- [ ] get involved in matters that don't concern them.
- [ ] expects cats to sleep all the time.
- [ ] disturb cats when they are sleeping.
- [ ] give people reasons to be curious.

Drawing Conclusions **21**

Drawing Conclusions — Introduction

Drawing conclusions is an advanced reading skill. It requires you to make a judgment about what you have read. It involves finding the **main idea** (p. 7), **making inferences** (p. 13) and using **context clues** (p. 17). It is related to other reading skills such as understanding **fact and opinion** (p. 43) and being able to distinguish between **relevant and irrelevant information** (p. 39).

A conclusion is reached by reasoning (thinking about a situation). It may require you having an opinion or making a decision. Drawing conclusions can only be done after you have read the whole extract (or story) — when you have all the information. It comes at the end — at the conclusion.

Read this extract from *That Proverbial Cat* by Elizabeth Best.

The next-door neighbour's garden was like a jungle — thickly overgrown with trees and shrubs. An old, old woman lived there alone. Some people said she was over one hundred years old. And others said she was a witch. Darin knew that could not be true because he did not believe in witches.

'Tiger! Tiger!' he called softly, but only the gentle stirring of wind among the leaves answered him.

'Well,' Darin thought. 'Am I going to stalk Tiger as I planned or am I going to become scared at the very first bit of danger? And what's to be scared of, anyway? An old woman I could beat running any day.'

So Darin convinced himself that he must follow Tiger into the overgrown jungle garden and bring him safely home.

Leaping for the top of the fence, he hauled himself over and dropped as quietly as he could down onto the other side.

Here he waited a moment, listening for any movements of either Tiger or the old woman and peering intently through the thick shrubs.

Nothing stirred.

He was about to take a step forward when a great crashing and flapping in the trees above him broke the silence.

His heart nearly jumped out of his body.

But it was only two magpies fighting over a plum. He looked through the thick weave of leaves towards the back of the house where he could just catch a glimpse of a small section of the back door and a concrete porch. He noticed that the door stood half open.

---

1. Darin is not as brave a person as he would like to believe. List two things Darin does that helps you to draw this conclusion. _____

_____

2. What information leads you to the conclusion that Darin was a little scared of the yard next door? (give one example) _____

3. Darin could be best described as (**cowardly**   **cautious**   **disinterested**). (circle one answer)

4. A good title for the extract would be (**The Magpies**   **Looking for Tiger**). (circle one answer)

Answers   1. he has to talk himself into going into the garden/the birds scare him, 2. he hides in the bushes OR he doesn't want to disturb the old lady, 3. cautious, 4. Looking for Tiger

22 Excel Comprehension Skillbuilder Year 5

Drawing Conclusions — Own Up!

by Ellen Robertson

The children were angry.

One boy at the back of the room banged the desk with his fist. Mrs Lovejoy had specifically promised him a science fiction book.

'Silence!' thundered Mrs McSnorty.

Steve and Suzie were deep in thought. Strangely, they were both remembering a story Mrs Lovejoy had read to them at the beginning of the year. It was about using the power of thought to change things. In fact, the children in the story had even used their power to shrink someone.

But what had their special words been? Finally, Suzie remembered. She whispered to her partner, 'Everyone think *Shrink, Stinker! — pass it on.*'

Then it ran around the room like a miniature railway: *Shrink, Stinker! Shrink, Stinker! Shrink, Stinker!*

Within minutes, all shuffling and fidgeting had stopped. The children sat, hands neatly folded on their desks, staring intently at their teacher.

Just then, the principal poked her head in. It appeared there was no problem after all. Obviously, Mrs Lovejoy had been exaggerating again. What could one expect? She had such a vivid imagination. The principal walked on.

Mrs McSnorty became suspicious. She was peering at the children over her wire-rimmed glasses, when suddenly she discovered that she could only just see over the top of the desk. It towered above her, like Everest.

She found herself scrambling around on her chair, which now loomed as large as a football oval. She shrieked, but she sounded like a mouse.

1. Circle the sentences that let you draw the conclusion that Mrs McSnorty was not liked by the children. (You might have to read the extract again.)

   (A) Mrs McSnorty shrieked, but she sounded like a mouse.

   (B) The principal poked her head in to check on the class.

   (C) Mrs McSnorty shouted at the class to be quiet.

   (D) One boy at the back of the room banged the desk with his fist.

2. What information leads you to the conclusion that Mrs McSnorty was being too strict? (give one reason) _____

3. The class could best be described as (rebelling   fearful). (circle your choice) What information helps you make this conclusion? (tick your reasons)

   ☐ They did exactly as they were told.

   ☐ They all secretly agreed to take action.

   ☐ Mrs Lovejoy was going to read a book.

   ☐ One student thumped the desk.

   ☐ The principal checked on the class.

   ☐ Mrs McSnorty became suspicious.

4. This is meant to be a humorous story. Give an incident from the extract that lets you draw the conclusion that it's not serious. _____

5. You can conclude that the students got on well together.   True ☐   False ☐

Drawing Conclusions — Stevie Comes To Stay

by Gordon Winch

5 Forest Way
Beecroft
SUNDAY

Dear Joel,

Just a short letter to tell you we got here O.K. Thanks for seeing us off. WOW, this is an upside-down place! I guess that's why they call it down-under. You know how cold it was in Madison and Chicago when we left, snow on the road and all. Well, it was

R E D H O T

when we landed. I was boiling in my jacket. I sure took it off fast.

And you know what? They drive cars on the wrong side of the road. It's a ~~wunder~~ wonder there aren't more accidents.

I couldn't understand the cab driver at first. Aussies sure talk with funny voices. He kept saying, 'You'll loik it here mite'. He meant 'You'll LIKE it here MATE' (I think). They call everyone 'mite' (mate). It means 'buddy'. But why don't they say so? I guess it's down-under talk.

Our house has no basement. Wonder where they play when it snows. Oops, there's no snow in ~~Sidney~~ Sydney. Wouldn't you bet? It's not a bad house though. Some great trees to climb in the garden. They call them gum trees, the taxi driver said. Bet you'd be in ~~trubble~~ trouble if you tried to chew the gum from them. It would stick your teeth together.

I'll write next week.

Stevie.

1. Circle the information that lets you draw the conclusion that this is Stevie's first trip to Australia. (You might have to read the extract again.)

   (A) Stevie was amused by the way the taxi driver spoke.

   (B) Stevie made several spelling mistakes in his letter.

   (C) Stevie observed that Australians drove on the 'wrong side' of the road.

   (D) Stevie had to take his jacket off because he was hot.

   (E) Stevie came to Australia by plane.

2. What information leads you to the conclusion that Stevie expected snow in Sydney?

   (give one reason) _____

3. Stevie (was   was not) happy about being in Australia. (circle your choice) What information helps you make this conclusion? (tick your reasons)

   ☐ Stevie had trees to climb in the yard.   ☐ The new house had no basement.

   ☐ He was amused by the taxi driver's talk.   ☐ It was very hot when they landed.

4. You can conclude that Stevie had friends in the United States.   True ☐   False ☐

24 Excel Comprehension Skillbuilder Year 5

Drawing Conclusions — Masakuni and the Bees

by David Shapiro

Masakuni was a mighty warrior. He was the Emperor's friend and often led the Emperor's men in battle, fighting fiercely to defend the Emperor.

Once it happened that the mighty Masakuni met his own cousin, Kiza, in battle. Kiza had rebelled against the Emperor, thinking to become ruler over all Japan.

Kiza had ten times as many men fighting for him in that battle. Most of the Emperor's men were killed or captured — except the mighty Masakuni, who hid, along with what was left of his army, in a valley called Kizagawa.

Here the monstrous mountains towered high above the valley. Cliffs were cut from rugged rock and fell straight into the valley floor where streams ran as fast as silver light.

Masakuni and his army held out month after month. But one day Masakuni's lookouts fell asleep, and Kiza's soldiers struck and killed most of Masakuni's men. Masakuni and a few survivors slipped then into a hidden cave and remained there.

Kiza knew his cousin crouched somewhere, hiding in among the thick green of the valley. Vexed, impatient, Kiza waited to kill his cousin.

Masakuni and his men, who were seven altogether, sat in silence, in the darkness, buried deeply in the rock, surrounded by shadows.

1. Masakuni was a brave person. Tick the boxes next to the information that lets you draw this conclusion. (You might have to read the extract again.)

☐ Masakuni fought a larger army. ☐ Masakuni was the Emperor's friend.

☐ Kiza was Masakuni's cousin. ☐ Most of Masakuni's soldiers died.

☐ Masakuni was a mighty warrior. ☐ Masakuni's army hid in a valley.

2. What information leads you to the conclusion that Kiza really wanted Masakuni dead? (give one reason) _____

3. Kiza could be best described as a (brave   determined   careless) person.

4. Masakuni's decision to hide could best be described as (cunning necessary reckless).

5. Masakuni would most likely (lose   win) the next battle. (circle one word). What information leads you to this conclusion? (tick all the boxes you need)

☐ Kiza was a greater warrior. ☐ Masakuni had only seven men left.

☐ The Emperor trusted Masakuni. ☐ Masakuni's lookout fell asleep.

6. You can conclude that the valley was a good hiding place.   True ☐   False ☐

7. You can conclude that Masakuni remained loyal to the Emperor.   True ☐   False ☐

8. You can conclude that Kiza was a merciful warrior.   True ☐   False ☐

Noting Detail — Introduction

Detail plays an important part in written works. Details help to give the reader a clear understanding of the story or the topic. Details can give different types of writing its particular 'flavour'. Details often allow the reader to draw conclusions (see p. 29).When looking at details we must determine whether or not they are appropriate (see **Relevant and irrelevant information** p. 39).

Look at this extract from *That Proverbial Cat* by Elizabeth Best.

So Darin made a vow to himself that from now on he would be far more careful in the protection of his beloved cat.

Darin gave up a lot of time to play with Tiger while the cat was confined indoors. Then at last the bandage was taken off, the claw was cured and Tiger was free to roam again where he would.

We read that Darin is looking out for his cat, Tiger. The detail can give us some understanding of the type of person Darin is.

1. What 'details' suggest that Darin is caring of Tiger? The details that tell us this are: Darin gave up his own time (probably playing time) to play with Tiger; Darin vowed (promised) to be careful protecting Tiger.

2. What 'detail' suggests that Darin had not always been as caring as he should have been? **Suggested answer.** Darin vowed **from now on** he would be more careful which suggests that he hadn't been as careful as he would have liked in the past.

3. What detail suggests that Tiger had hurt a leg? _____

_____

Read the next extract from *That Proverbial Cat*.

Once again Darin prepared himself to guard and protect Tiger against the cat's now quite insatiable curiosity.

And so it all began again.

Tiger, after inspecting his paw, so recently unbandaged, gave it a bit of a lick over and was ready to go. Moving steadily, his body rolling gracefully, he walked to the side fence where the lower part of the paling was broken off.

---

4. What action of Tiger tells the reader that Tiger knew where he was going? _____

_____

5. Tiger's injury had no after-effects. What detail tells the reader this? _____

_____

Answers

1 and 2. These were done for you. 3. Tiger was confined indoors which implies he couldn't walk. Taking off the bandage Darin saw that the claw was cured. Tiger could roam again. 4. Tiger went straight for the hole in the fence. 5. Tiger didn't limp or stagger. He moved steadily.

Noting Detail — Time Capsule

by Rachael Collison

They had reached the old ghost town of Caranyah. What a strange place it was. Once a lively township, where men and women rushed to find gold, where hawkers and traders flocked from China, India, and England. Caranyah was deserted now.

Buildings stood in various stages of decay and disrepair. Weeds grew everywhere as the bush crept in to reclaim the town. Wooden planks littered the ground or swung from broken frames. An occasional creak could be heard, as though the pitiful small huts were about to fall over.

Anne stood still, looking around in wonder. In spite of the eerie atmosphere, she was not at all afraid. She felt rather excited, indeed, and her heart was beating faster.

Cousin Elizabeth was right. This was the place!

James leant against a tree, his arms folded. He had the peculiar feeling that he was about to discover some strange secret.

Suddenly they seemed to hear singing. It was not a song they knew, and yet it sounded vaguely familiar. Voices echoed faintly around them, singing in words they could not understand. A wild kind of wailing sound it was, high and thin, carried through the air like a reed being played by the winds.

James and Anne whirled around. Where was that singing coming from?

They realised then that Cousin Elizabeth had disappeared — just like that.

1. Draw lines from '**Old Caranyah**' and '**Present day Caranyah**' to details that describe the town at those times.

   Old Caranyah

   people from China

   eerie atmosphere

   many traders

   Present day Caranyah

   wooden planks littering the ground

   weeds everywhere

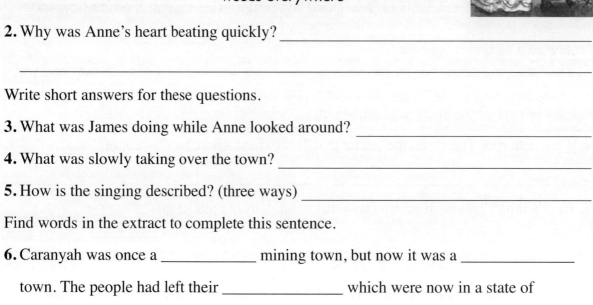

2. Why was Anne's heart beating quickly? _____

_____

Write short answers for these questions.

3. What was James doing while Anne looked around? _____

4. What was slowly taking over the town? _____

5. How is the singing described? (three ways) _____

Find words in the extract to complete this sentence.

6. Caranyah was once a _____ mining town, but now it was a _____ town. The people had left their _____ which were now in a state of _____. Many _____ houses were about to fall over.

Noting Detail **27**

Noting Detail — The Secret Of Yesterday Hills

by Elsie Young

The Difficult Journey

Galahs flapped away from the approaching buzz of the bicycle wheels, and the budgerigars shot up like green rockets from the roadside clumps of dry spinifex. Crows roamed the skies with their lonely, drawn out cries. The country was all flat, not a hill or a rise anywhere, and the red empty road rolled away under the bike wheels. No one talked much after the first hour. The spring day became warmer and the sun leant heavily on their shoulders.

Perry looked over at Colin and wondered again why he'd been so against taking them to the mysterious hills. And now that they were on their way, was it going to be worth the effort? He yawned.

They ate their lunch in a dried up river course under immense red gums that waited patiently for the rain. As they went on, the country changed. Soon there were no gidgee or beefwood or any other big trees. Only mulga. More and more of it — on both sides of the road, and ahead, and closing in behind. Dark-limbed, smallish trees with narrow grey-green leaves — an acacia, Colin had told them one day. In really bad droughts it was 'rolled' or bulldozed as feed for starving sheep.

How awful to be lost in there, Perry was thinking when suddenly Colin headed off the road and into it, waving them after him. Perry hesitated. He didn't want to leave that red friendly road and go in amongst all that grey, silent bush.

'Come on!' yelled Frank, and Perry put his wheels in motion again and followed the others. Janice turned and grinned at him.

The trees looked ancient with their dry, wrinkled bark. Birds didn't seem to like them — there was not a sound to be heard from the branches above. At least the trees weren't as thick as they had seemed from the road and there was no undergrowth to push through, but dead, spiky branches lay around and there were patches of grey, thorny weed.

They followed a narrow, twisted path between the trees. 'All that's left of the old sheep track,' Colin said. Everyone concentrated on keeping the wheels moving; panting and pushing down hard on the pedals. It was very hard going.

1. Draw a line to match the details that go with the plants.

red gums	patches of grey
acacias	dry river course
thorny weeds	feed for sheep

2. Choose the best way to complete this sentence. (Tick the correct box.)
When they left the road

☐ they got off their bicycles. ☐ they ate their lunch in a dry river course.

☐ the bush became quiet.

3. Gidgee is the name of a type of parrot. True ☐ False ☐

4. Once the riders left the road they were quickly lost. True ☐ False ☐

5. Galahs were frightened by the green rockets from the spinifex. True ☐ False ☐

6. Name the four people mentioned in the extract. _____

Noting Detail — Rainforests

by Stephen Jones

Details are important in factual texts. Details can be useful when doing research projects.

Tropical rainforests cover only six percent of the Earth's land surface, yet it is believed that they are home for half the world's living species. More species of all kinds live in rainforests than anywhere else on earth — but every one and a half seconds rainforest equal to a football field in size is destroyed.

Their destruction is a major cause of the rising greenhouse gas levels in the atmosphere. Even more importantly, it puts them at the centre of one the most important but least publicised crises we face today. Put simply, human activity, particularly clearing of tropical rainforest, is responsible for the greatest period of extinction for 65 million years.

Although this abuse is enormous, we can still be reasonably confident that life on Earth will recover. It has in the past — but this has taken millions of years. However, for the children of today and the citizens of tomorrow the destruction of our rainforests is a calamity. A vast irreplaceable treasure-house of foods and medicines is being bulldozed away; a spring of knowledge and beauty is drying up. If we ignore what is happening, this precious resource will be lost forever.

To help us know more, so that we can help save our rainforests, we need to look at some background topics that are important for understanding rainforests.

1. Tick the box that is **NOT** a description of a rainforest.

☐ a treasure-house of foods

☐ rising greenhouse gas levels in the atmosphere

☐ cover six percent of the Earth's land surface

☐ home to half the world's living species

2. Tick the boxes that give details about the destruction of rainforests.

☐ many important medicines may be lost   ☐ the earth can never recover

☐ greenhouse conditions will get worse   ☐ the rate of destruction is very fast

3. To help save rainforests we need to know more about them.   True ☐ False ☐

4. Rainforests are being destroyed because they are drying up.   True ☐ False ☐

5. Greenhouse gases are causing changes in the atmosphere.   True ☐ False ☐

6. It is most likely that our children will be able to enjoy rainforests. True ☐ False ☐

7. Clearing of rainforests in an important way of getting more food. True ☐ False ☐

8. The saving of rainforests is the responsibility of (**farmers   all citizens   footballers bulldozer drivers**). (Circle one answer)

9. The details give the reader some idea of what rainforest destruction is like. How would you describe countries that allow the destruction of rainforests? _____

LIFT-OUT
ANSWER SECTION

A2 Excel Comprehension Skillbuilder Year 5

Answers

Page 1: Finding Facts — Introduction: Paddock for a Pony by Elizabeth Best
1. Deborah, Pat and Billy were building the tree house.
2. They saw other children (slip quietly away).
3. Mr Crunkhorn threatened the children with a stick and threatened to tell their parents.
4. behind the fence.

Page 2: Strange Mysteries by Rachael Collinson
1. Uri first surprised his mother when he was three years old.
2. Uri surprised his mother when he bent spoons by staring at them.
3. True   4. True   5. False   6. True   7. magnet
8. (d) magnet needles moved

Page 3: Tell me How by Mike Callaghan, Peter Knapp, Ross Latham and Peter Sloan
1. three types of ants.   2. when it is time to build a new nest.
3. How is a new colony started?
4. True   5. True   6. False   7. female/female workers

Page 4: The Portland Fairy Penguins by Edel Wignell
1. of natural causes.   2. have banded penguins for many years.
3. Fairy penguins make good pets.   4. True   5. False
6. Answer will vary. Possible answers: so they can make sure the colony is not becoming endangered, so they can record their habits.

Page 5: The Sylvia Mystery by Penny Hall
1. none   2. into the pool.   3. gaol.   4. bored   5. False   6. False
7. Trees blocked the view of the other houses.

Page 6: What a Waste! by Stephen Jones
1. Most household rubbish —— a new way of dealing with rubbish.
   Recycling is —— can be recycled.
   When we recycle waste —— we use it to make new products.
2. The extract is about the history and current state of recycling.   3. deposit   4. False
5. True   6. Answers will vary.   7. ordinary householders.

Page 7: Finding the Main Idea — Introduction: What a Waste! by Stephen Jones
1. 3   2. 3   3. 3   4. The Problem of Waste
5. Recycling is increasing.   6. True

Page 8: Time Capsule by Rachael Collinson
1. paragraph 6   2. This is a story about time.   3. Everything seemed normal.
4. Suggested answer: Anne has a mysterious feeling.   5. Strange Feelings
6. False   7. False

Page 9: Battlers of the Great Depression by Edel Wignell
1. 5   2. America was prosperous in the 1920s.
3. People had no money because they could not find work.
4. According to the extract life was difficult for the period 1929 to 1950.
5. Second World War   6. Years of Difficulty
7. The disaster had an effect worldwide.   8. False

Page 10: Made For Australia by Judith Kendra
1. Paragraph 1
2. Paragraph 1 —— development of solar power cells
   Paragraph 2 —— importance of solar power for Australia
   Paragraph 3 —— how solar heating works
3. Power for the Future.   4. Paragraph 3   5. (A) supplying solar power to factories
6. False   7. True   8. Electricity costs more in the country than the city.

Page 11: Saving Wildlife by Edel Wignell
1. 9   2. The decoys were very lifelike.   3. Saving the Gannets.   4. True

Answers **A3**

5. False   6. encouraging gannets to return to their island nesting grounds   7. Cat Island

Page 12: My Neighbours at Nagin by Judy Parker
1. the origins (beginnings) of houseboats in Kashmir 2. the interior (inside) of a houseboat.
3. where houseboat owners live.   4. True   5. True   6. False
7. Doongas are flat, plain houseboats where Kashmiri houseboat owners live.
8. supporting detail   9. cedar

Page 13: Making Inferences — Introduction: The Sylvia Mystery by Penny Hall
1. Suggested answer. No adult voice bellowed in disapproval when she tossed her can into the pool. (Other answers are possible.)
2. Kat didn't use the pool without permission.   3. It is a huge house with many electronic gadgets

Page 14: The Incredible Experience of Megan Kingsley by Pamela O'Connor
1. Megan is having a bad dream (nightmare).
2. The night had been cold, Megan needs to dry off after getting wet.
3. throwing stones at her.   4. False   5. False

Page 15: The Secret of Yesterday Hills by Elsie Young
1. enjoyed where he had been living. 2. living in a small country town.   3. False   4. False
5. Suggested answer: he was trying to hide his sick feeling from his parents.   6. uncooperative.
7. (B) the orange drink

Page 16: Own Up! by Ellen Robertson
1. has been involved in a strange incident   2. something was happening she didn't understand
3. True   4. False
5. **Suggested answer**. They had been involved in the disappearance of Mrs McSnorty.   6. thoughtful

Page 17: Using Context Clues — Introduction: Going Fishing With My Dad
        by Jan Weeks
1. going fishing
2. Not very often or never. Reasons: The son thought it would be the greatest fun. He hadn't gone on the last trip. He had to pester his father to take him.
3. pestering   4. False

Page 18: Not Zackly by Mary Small
1. Bandit is most likely a dog.   2. the children only had limited time to enjoy themselves
3. the creek might be in flood.   4. Julie was leaving the house to walk to the creek.
5. Bandit rushed to the front door when Leigh said the word 'walk'.   6. had blue patches

Page 19: Show Off by Hazel Edwards
1. a) spilt glue on the gym floor; b) got struck on the roof when collecting tennis balls; (OR fell off the ladder into the Grade 2 herb garden)
2. He was compared unfavourably with Amanda.   3. spider   4. good fun
5. Matthew will cause some sort of disaster to happen.   6. False (the cousin is Matthew)   7. False

Page 20: That Proverbial Cat by Elizabeth Best
1. The cat became curious about Darin.
2. The cat's reaction to Darin lying on the floor was unexpected.   3. style   4. as a result
5. True   6. True
7. a) pretended to be asleep (disinterested); b) watched the cat closely
8. get involved in matters that don't concern them.

Page 21: Drawing Conclusions — Introduction: That Proverbial Cat by Elizabeth Best
1. he had to convince himself he was not scared / the flapping birds frightened him / he hides in the bushes / he calls the garden a jungle
2. he was nervous about hiding in the garden (jungle) / he didn't want to disturb the old lady, who was known as a witch
3. Darin could best be described as cautious.   4. Looking for Tiger

Page 22: Own Up! by Ellen Robertson
1. (B) The principal poked her head in to check on the class (implied that Mrs Lovejoy had warned her there might be a problem). (D) One boy at the back of the room banged the desk with his fist.

A4   Excel Comprehension Skillbuilder Year 5

2. She shouted at the class.
3. The class could best be described as **rebelling**.
   One student thumped the desk. They all secretly agreed to take action.
4. Mrs McSnorty is turned into a very small person.   5. True

Page 23: Stevie Comes To Stay by Gordon Winch
1. (A) Stevie was amused by the way the taxi driver spoke. (C) Stevie observed that Australians drove on the 'wrong side' of the road.
2. He was wearing a jacket; he was surprised there was no basement in his house (necessary if it snows).
3. Stevie was happy about being in Australia.
   Stevie had trees to climb in the yard. He was amused by the taxi driver's talk.   4. True

Page 24: Masakuni and the Bees by David Shapiro
1. Masakuni fought a larger army. Masakuni was a mighty warrior.
2. Even though Masakuni had only a few men left, Kiza waited for months to catch him.
3. Kiza could best be described as a determined person.
4. Masakuni's decision to hide could best be described as necessary.
5. Masakuni would most likely lose the next battle.
   Masakuni had only seven men left.
6. True   7. True   8. False

Page 25: Noting Detail — Introduction: That Proverbial Cat by Elizabeth Best
1. The details that tell us this are: Darin gave up his own time (probably playing time) to play with Tiger; Darin vowed (promised) to be careful protecting Tiger.
2. **Suggested answer.** Darin vowed **from now on** he would be more careful which suggests that he hadn't been as careful as he would have liked in the past.
3. Tiger was confined indoors which implies he couldn't walk. Taking off the bandage Darin saw that the claw was cured. Tiger could roam again.
4. Tiger went straight for the hole in the fence.
5. Tiger didn't limp or stagger. He moved steadily.

Page 26: Time Capsule by Rachael Collison
1.
   Old Caranyah — people from China
   — eerie atmosphere
   — many traders
   Present day Caranyah — wooden planks littering the ground
   — weeds everywhere
2. Anne felt excited.   3. leaning against a tree (with his arms folded)   4. the bush
5. familiar, high, thin, (like wailing) 6. gold, ghost, homes, decay (disrepair), small

Page 27: The Secret of Yesterday Hills by Elsie Young
1. red gums — patches of grey
   acacias — dry river course
   thorny weeds — feed for sheep
2. the bush became quiet.   3. False   4. False   5. False
6. Perry, Colin, Frank, Janice

Page 28: Rainforests by Stephen Jones
1. rising greenhouse gas levels in the atmosphere
2. many important medicines may be lost; greenhouse conditions will get worse; the rate of destruction is very fast
3. True   4. False   5. True   6. False   7. False   8. all citizens
9. Answers will vary.

Page 29: Following Directions — Introduction: What's Cooking? by Kerri Bingle, David Bowden and Jenny Dibley
1. 6 (steps)   2. 6 (different ingredients)   3. 6 (people)   4. corn chips   5. dip
6. An entree is usually served **before** the main meal.

Page 30: Puppets by Carole Hooper
1. 5   2. about 10   3. (dowel) rod   4. To make a papier-mâché puppet.

Answers A5

5. First take half a large sheet of newspaper and **scrunch** it into a ball.
6. It will take few (several) days to complete a papier-mâché puppet.
7. attach a body made from material   8. False   9. False   10. True

Page 31: What's Cooking? by Kerri Bingle, David Bowden and Jenny Dibley
1. 5   2. 6   3. pitta   4. cucumber
5. This recipe makes enough tzatziki for many people to taste.
6. Tzatziki is eaten by dipping raw vegetables/pitta bread in it.   7. This is a recipe for an entree.
8. 4 Cool mixture in a fridge.
   1 Peel a cucumber.
   3 Mix the cucumber with yoghurt and spices.
   2 Grate the cucumber.
10. Now you have a great party starter!

Page 32: The Age of Dinosaurs in Australia by Tim Flannery and Paula Kendall
1. a) latex b) plaster   2. 5
3. The latex is used to make a (detailed) mould.
4. Before removing the bone from the cast, the plaster must be set hard. 5. False

Page 33: Understanding Questions — Introduction: Rainforests
     by Stephen Jones
1. You could find many different species of trees in a tropical rainforest.
2. Trees of the same species ——— the most common rainforest plants.
  The wind does not blow ——— can be separated by large distances.
  Flowering plants are ——— inside the jungle canopy.
3. False   4. a) Birds, insects and mammals can all be **pollinators**.
              b) **Angiosperms** is another name for flowering plants.

Page 34: KID$ With Working Idea$ by Hazel Edwards

1.

Luke				Troy		
dams	yabbies	nets		papers	night	bike
summer	lines	weekends		letter boxes	milk crate	

1. Troy   2. about $1.10   3. after school and weekends
4. Troy likes ——— of papers on Wednesday nights.
  Trucks drop big bundles ——— riding his bike around the streets.
  Matthew and Luke go yabbying——— after school and on weekends.
5. Troy and Luke could be described as being energetic.   6. Answers will vary

Page 35: Understanding Questions — Cloze exercises

That Proverbial Cat by Elizabeth Best
Tiger's paws were so sore for the next three days that he willingly stayed around the house. Darin **stayed** with him. He was full of guilt. Once again his **efforts** to protect his cat had caused him injury.
   Early one morning, when Tiger's sore paws were less tender to **walk** on, he made a tour of the garden, and when Darin turned his head for a moment, managed to disappear completely.

Own up! by Ellen Robinson
Dinner was cooking on the stove. It was a gas **stove**, so there were always plenty of matches around. The stew was bubbling away fiercely. What if the matchbox fell into the **stew**? Dreadful thought. Susie quickly reached up to grab the matchbox.
   Her hand **touched** it when her mother suddenly came in from the yard and banged the door.

Going Fishing with my Dad by Jan Weeks
Dad stood with his oar upright in the river, and was surprised to discover how **shallow** the water was. Only about waist deep. We could **push** the boat downstream.
   I didn't mind. It was like we were having our own **adventure**.
   'You know something, Dad?' I said paddling, beside him. 'Fishing's the greatest fun.'

A6 Excel Comprehension Skillbuilder Year 5

Page 36: **Understanding Questions — Multiple choice questions: Sport in the Making — Tennis** by Shane Power

1. (A) indoors as well as outdoor.　　2. (C) France.　　3. (D) people began betting on it.
4. 3　Players used a short handled bat.
   1　A glove was used to hit the ball.
   4　Tennis was played in England.
   2　Strings were stretched across the glove.

Page 37: **Understanding Paragraphs — Introduction: Own Up!** by Ellen Robertson

1. a 2,　b. 1,　c. 4,　d. 3,　e. 1,　f. 2;
2. Just then　　　3. an important event is happening　4. The main person in paragraph 9 is Mrs McSnorty.

Page 38: **Understanding Paragraphs — 2**

Note: Indenting has been included to help you.

The Incredible Experience of Megan Kingsley by Pamela O'Connor

> It was a fine, hot January night. The light breeze could hardly be felt and caused only faint stirrings in the trees every now and then.
>
> Aurora was already at the cubby house, shaking her head in amusement as Megan and Patrick, loaded down with food, sleeping bags and assorted paraphernalia, staggered down the path. Aurora, as usual, had brought nothing with her.
>
> Later they laid out the sleeping bags and placed the food and other things in the corner of the room where Patrick was going to sleep. He objected loudly but Megan pointed out that as he was the smallest person in there, the least he could do was to make way for a few small items.

The Sylvia Mystery by Penny Hall

> The next morning, right on time, Kat was up the ladder propped against the back fence. She peered through the trees but there was nothing to be seen. She made herself as comfortable as she could and prepared to wait.
>
> From above her head there came a little, breathy giggle, and a voice whispered, 'I'm up here.' Kat peered up the densely leafed branches overhead.
>
> 'Where? I can't see you.'

Legends of our Land by Oodgeroo Noonuccal

> Before the whites came, the Noonuccal Tribe roamed free over their territory, going on walkabouts, continually on the move, searching for food.
>
> One day they decided to go to the northernmost part of the island, which they called Minjerribah.
>
> Now there was an old woman of the tribe who was always complaining. This day she was nagging the tribe about food, that she never got enough or it was poor quality and that the tribe treated her badly all the time. The tribal elders got very angry with her and told her to stop complaining but she would not.
>
> Finally the elders ordered her to be tied to a stake in the ground at the far end of the island. They told her they would return with food and left her, still growling.

Going Fishing with my Dad by Jan Weeks

> 'Caught anything?' Dad asked.
>
> One of them held up a couple of fish as long as my arm.
>
> Dad's eyes almost popped out. Flathead! And in the bottom of their boat they had at least a dozen more, all about the same size. They had been caught upriver.
>
> 'You having any luck here?' they asked.
>
> Dad shook his head but couldn't resist telling them about the one that got away, only this time it weighed four kilos, possibly five.
>
> 'It was probably a whale!' I said, loudly enough for Dad to hear.

Answers **A7**

Page 39: Relevant and Irrelevant Information — Introduction:

Tell me How by Mike Callaghan, Peter Knapp, Ross Latham and Peter Sloan
1. Ants are more numerous than any other animal.
2. To understand ants we must first understand that they are social animals.

Page 40: Not Zackly by Mary Small
1. Being allowed to join in helps people to feel accepted for what they are. Nicknames can make people feel rejected. To improve cricket skills, it is important to practise.
2. unsporting, quarrelsome, lazy   3. bossy, selfish, offensive
4. Zachary was asked to join in the game of cricket.   5. Zachary scores one run in cricket.

Page 41: Show Off by Hazel Edwards
1. The children passed rows of different cakes.   2. spiteful, selfish, keen   3. determined, anxious
4. Matthew knows who won the prize for the best carrot cake.   5. False
6. True   7. True (includes the narrator)

Page 42: Paddock for a Pony by Elizabeth Best
1. Pat and Deborah walked home in silence. (so excited they hardly dared to speak). Pat and Deborah threw their bags onto the lawn.
2. The guinea pig had had babies (and Deborah was going to see them for the first time).
3. stubborn, upset, angry, rough   4. excited, happy
5. (D) She holds a baby guinea pig in her hands.

Page 43: Fact and Opinion — Introduction: Radio Current Affairs by Elizabeth Halley
1. Fact   2. Opinion   3. Fact   4. Fact

Page 44: Battlers of the Great Depression by Edel Wignell
1. Housework was drudgery.   2. Understanding the difficulties of the time.

Made for Australia by Judith Kendra
1. Scientists came to Australia from Britain and Europe. The slide raft was invented by Qantas.
2. it is fair to say   3. True

Page 45: Not Another Ad! by John D. Fitzgerald
1. The unwanted material can often be seen blowing around the streets. When we are going away we can cancel deliveries of newspapers. Many people complain about advertising material left in their letterboxes.
2. True   3. True   4. Answers will vary.
5. Suggested answers: Do a survey. Look for NO JUNK MAIL signs on letterboxes.
6. Answers will vary. Suggested answer: The home owner can't be bothered collecting it.
7. Police station OR insurance company   8. True

Page 46: Fact and Opinion — My Diary by Jenny Jarman-Walker
1. Mr Davis doesn't talk much, which is good.
2. This writing comes from a **diary** which should prepare the reader for writing that contains facts as well as **opinions**.
3. True   4. True   5. False   6. This is a fact.
7. It is a fact that the diary writer is **about to start work**.

Page 47: Understanding Persuasion — Introduction
1. yourself (this could be you!)   2. Uniting people across oceans   3. False

Page 48: What a Waste! by Stephen Jones
1. to politicians   2. you, us   3. hopeful, motivated
4. Not to make use of your imagination would be the worst waste of all.
5. He uses a heading that makes the reader think the article is important.

Page 49: Saving Wildlife by Edel Wignell
1. Destruction of rainforests means death for many of species of fauna. People try to restore the habitat, but this is impossible.
2. needs everyone's attention.   3. angry, informed, motivated
4. The heading is used to arouse the reader's attention.   5. True   6. False   7. False

A8 Excel Comprehension Skillbuilder Year 5

Page 50: Going Fishing with my Dad by Jan Weeks
1. embarrassing his father, pestering his father, being helpful around the house
2. agreed, without giving a definite time to go   3. False   4. False
5. Answers may vary. I think he would have kept pestering because he really wanted to go fishing.
6. The narrator's actions probably annoyed the father.

Page 51: **Understanding and Using Tables of Contents — Introduction**
Table of Contents from Puppets by Carole Hooper
1. page 21   2. Some special puppets from around the world   3. True   4. True
5. True   6. Bibliography,
7. The **Introduction** is at the front of the book. The **Bibliography** is at the back.

Page 52: Understanding and Using Tables of Contents — What a Waste! by Stephen Jones
1. page 61   2. page 31   3. How much do we waste, how much do we recycle?
4. In the index.   5. How to pronounce (say) unusual or difficult words used in the text
6. in the front   7. True   8. True   9. page 8 (Waste through the ages)

Page 53: Understanding and Using an Index — Introduction: Not Another Ad! by John D. Fitzgerald
1. page 21   2. 2   3. environment   4. False   5. True   6. 53 (to p.54)

Page 54: Made For Australia by Judith Kendra
1. page 17   2. 2   3. page 35   4. page 47   5. False
6. It is a convention to put **The** last when it is in a title/heading. The other words are more important, and so many phrases start with 'The' the entry would be very long.
7. False   8. There are **references to Akubra hats on two different pages**.   9. False

Page 55: **Using Timetables — Introduction**
1. 12 noon   2. two hours   3. 3.30   4. 10.45   5. Picnic Park   6. Pavilion
7. half court basketball OR touch football   8. True   9. False

Page 56: Using Timetables — Train Timetables
1. three   2. 9.45   3. This is a timetable for every day except **Sunday**.
4. one   5. 8.10   6. 55 **minutes**.   7. 9.25
8. The longest part of the journey is between **Newtown** and **Lakemba**.
9. True   10. True   11. 8.40   12. four   13. It stops at less stations.

Page 57: **Understanding Maps — Introduction: What's Cooking?** by Kerri Bingle, David Bowden and Jenny Dibley
1. east   2. north   3. west   4. south   5. Timor Sea   6. about 1100 km
7. Australia's closest neighbour is **Papua New Guinea**.

Page 58: What's Cooking (Greece) by Kerri Bingle, David Bowden and Jenny Dibley (p. 9)
1. north   2. south   3. north   4. east   5. west   6. west
7. Austria   8. Bulgaria and Romania   9. Mediterranean Sea   10. 800 km.
11. False   12. False

Page 59: Understanding Graphs and Charts — Introduction: What a Waste by Stephen Jones
1. households   2. Most household rubbish is either **paper** or **food**.   3. True   4. True
5. grass clipping (other answers possible)   6. No

Page 60: Understanding Charts — The Portland Fairy Penguin by Edel Wignell
1. five   2. September (January chicks are the last for the season.)   3. 4 months
4. **Nest building** happens before **egg laying**.   5. False   6. False   7. False
8. nest building   9. The two activities that happen in July are **burrow attendance** and **nest building**.

Following Directions — Introduction

If we want to know how to do something, we have to follow **a procedure** or, to use another term, **follow directions**. You may have books at home that tell you how to do things. It might be how to make papier maché or how to bake a cake.

You will find many books that give directions in your school library; how to play sport, how to do magic tricks, how to knit, how to do science experiments, how to recycle waste materials, and so on. Many magazines give directions, from how to catch fish to how to care for your hair.

Some directions are simple. A machine at a ferry terminal has **instructions** on how to purchase a ticket. We call each part of the directions (instructions) **steps**.

Some directions have many steps. The directions for replacing a part in a car could be quite complex. People follow directions for something nearly every day of their lives.

Read the following set of simple instructions, a recipe from *What's Cooking? a children's guide to food from other lands* by Kerri Bingle, David Bowden and Jenny Dibley.

Guacamole ◄——————————— *The aim (what you will make)*
Guacamole is an entree or dip which is scooped out with corn chips.

Serves 6 ◄——————————— *How many people you will be catering for.*
Ingredients ◄——————————— *Often called the materials needed.*

2 ripe avocados
a little lemon juice
2 fresh tomatoes, finely chopped
½ an onion, finely chopped

1 chilli, finely chopped
2 tablespoons fresh coriander, finely chopped

Method ◄————————————— *What you do — the steps (or directions) you must follow.*

1. Mix all the ingredients except the avocados in a bowl.
2. Sprinkle with lemon juice.
3. Cut the avocados in half. Remove the stones and scoop out the flesh.
4. Add this to the mixture.
5. Mix briefly, leaving the mixture slightly coarse. (Do not use a food processor.)
6. Place into a serving bowl and serve with corn chips. ◄——————— *concluding step*

Note: Many recipes have a **concluding statement** — this could be a suggestion on how to present the food.

1. How many steps are there in making guacamole? (short answer) _____

2. How many different ingredients do you need to make guacamole? (short answer) _____

3. This recipe makes enough guacamole for _____ people.

4. What should guacamole be served with? _____ (short answer)

5. Guacamole is called a _____ because you dip chips in it to eat it.

6. An entree is usually served (**before**   **during**   **after**) the main meal. (circle one word)

Answers   1. 6 steps, 2. 6, 3. 6, 4. corn chips, 5. dip, 6. before

Following Directions — Puppets

by Carole Hooper

Some puppets are extremely complicated and very difficult to make. Others can be created easily and quickly from only a few materials.

Papier-mâché puppet

This type of puppet is basically a head on a stick. It is slightly more difficult to make and will take a few days to finish.

You will need:

sheets of newspaper   paste
scrap materials   paint
a stick or dowel rod

Method

First take half a large sheet of newspaper and scrunch it into a ball. Then tear a few long strips of newspaper and paste these around the ball to hold it in position. Push the stick or rod firmly into the ball. Then completely cover the ball with small pieces of well-pasted newspaper. Let this first layer dry before adding any more. When you add the second layer you can also make features such as a nose by building up certain areas with several pieces of newspaper.

After the second or third layer has dried, the puppet can be painted. Next the eyes, mouth, hair and so on, can be added. You can then make the puppet's body from a piece of fabric. This can be attached to the top of the stick using a rubber band.

Answer questions 1 to 3 with short answers.

1. How many different materials are needed to make a papier-mâché puppet? _____

2. About how many steps in the **method** for making a papier-mâché puppet? _____

3. What can be used instead of a stick when making a papier-mâché puppet? _____

4. Using your own words, explain what is the aim of these instructions? _____

_____

Find the missing words for each of these sentences.

5. First take half a large sheet of newspaper and _____ it into a ball.

6. It will take _____ days to complete a papier-mâché puppet.

7. Find the correct ending for this sentence.

The last step in making a papier-mâché puppet is to

☐ add a second or third layer of paper.   ☐ add the facial features (eyes, mouth, hair).

☐ let the puppet head dry completely.   ☐ attach a body made from material.

8. The nose is added when the eyes are added.   True ☐   False ☐

9. A rubber band is used to keep the head on.   True ☐   False ☐

10. You should wait before pasting a second layer of newspaper.   True ☐   False ☐

Following Directions — What's Cooking?
a children's guide to food from other lands

by Kerri Bingle, David Bowden and Jenny Dibley

Tzatziki

This is a dip eaten by Greek people before a meal. In Greece, tzatziki is usually eaten with bread. Australians often eat tzatziki with **pitta** bread (commonly known as Lebanese bread) or raw vegetables such as carrots and celery.

Serves: A taste for each member of the class

Ingredients

2 Lebanese or normal cucumbers
1 1/2 cups of Greek-style yoghurt
2 large crushed cloves of garlic

pepper to taste
juice of half a lemon
pinch of paprika

Method

1. Peel the skin from the cucumber
2. Grate the cucumber thinly
3. Mix the yoghurt, cucumber, crushed garlic, pepper, and a small amount of lemon juice.
4. Place in the refrigerator
5. When you are ready to serve the food sprinkle some paprika on the top

Answer questions 1 to 4 with short answers.

1. How many steps are there in making tzatziki? _____

2. How many different ingredients do you need to make tzatziki? _____

3. What is another name for Lebanese bread? _____

4. What is the main vegetable used in the making of tzatziki? _____

5. This recipe makes enough tzatziki for (two   a few   many) people to taste. (circle one word)

6. Tzatziki is eaten by dipping _____ in it.

7. This is a recipe for (an entree   main meal   sweet). (circle one word)

8. Number the boxes 1 to 4 to show the steps in order when making tzatziki.

☐ Cool mixture in a fridge.   ☐ Mix the cucumber with yoghurt and spices.

☐ Peel a cucumber.   ☐ Grate the cucumber.

9. A good **concluding statement** would be

☐ Make some more if you like it.   ☐ Keep a good supply of cucumbers.

☐ Now you have a great party starter!

Following Directions — The Age of Dinosaurs in Australia

by Tim Flannery and Paula Kendall

Cleaning dinosaur bones

This is sometimes necessary if a very delicate or valuable skeleton needs to be put on display, or if copies have to be sent to scientists overseas to make a cast*.

To make a cast a thin layer of latex is poured over the bone. This hardens to form a mould that reproduces every detail of the bone. Plaster is then poured over the latex to make the mould rigid. The original bone is then removed. Any number of replicas can be made by pouring plaster or fibreglass into the mould.

* a cast is a model or replica

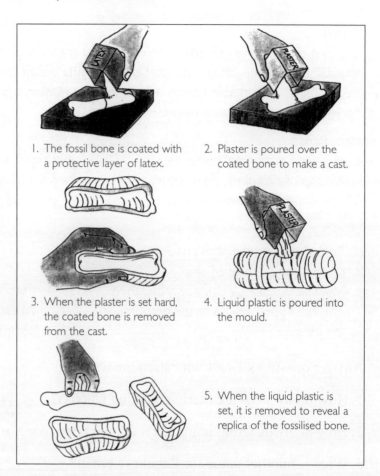

1. The fossil bone is coated with a protective layer of latex.
2. Plaster is poured over the coated bone to make a cast.
3. When the plaster is set hard, the coated bone is removed from the cast.
4. Liquid plastic is poured into the mould.
5. When the liquid plastic is set, it is removed to reveal a replica of the fossilised bone.

1. What are the two main materials needed to make a cast of a bone?

   a) _____ b) _____

2. How many steps are given for making a cast? (short answer) _____

3. What is the latex used for? _____

   _____

4. Before removing the bone from the cast, the plaster must be

   ☐ set hard.   ☐ easily broken off.   ☐ poured into the mould.

5. Pictures are used in the instructions to save space.   True ☐   False ☐

Understanding Questions — Introduction

In your comprehension exercises you will get many different types of questions. Different types of questions are used to see just how well you read and understand what you have read. You will get a number of different types of questions in this book.

Types of questions:
true–false questions (yes–no)
multiple choice questions
short answer questions
full sentence answer questions
matching exercises
sentence completing exercises
sequencing questions
labelling exercises
cloze exercises (filling in blanks)

- Questions that want you to **find information** may begin with how, when where or what. Sometimes you will be asked to give **names** or make **lists**.
- Questions that want you to **give a reason** will often begin with why.
- Some questions may ask you to **give an opinion**. For these questions you have to have your own ideas. These questions will ask you to **give answers in your own words**.
- Other questions may ask you to **search and find** information, especially in factual texts.

Read this extract and answer the questions.

Rainforests
by Stephen Jones

Ferns, lichen, algae and mosses are common in rainforests. However, **angiosperms** (flowering plants) are by far the most common type of plant. With so many species of trees growing in the tropical rainforest, trees of the same species are often separated by large distances.

As the wind does not blow inside the canopy, wind dispersal of pollen is impossible. To overcome this, flowering plants have evolved spectacular, fragrant and nectar-rich flowers which attract **pollinators** such as birds, insects and mammals to them. The pollinators are important because they enable pollination to take place over these long distances.

1. Where could you find many different species of trees? (full sentence answer)

_____

2. Draw a line to match these sentence beginnings with their right endings.

Trees of the same species   the most common rainforest plants.

The wind does not blow   can be separated by large distances.

Flowering plants are   inside the jungle canopy.

3. True or False. The wind spreads most rainforest pollen. True ☐ False ☐ (tick one box)

4. Complete these sentences. a) Birds, insects and mammals can all be _____.

             b) _____ is another name for flowering plants.

Answers 1. You could find many different species of trees in a tropical rainforest. 2. Trees of the same species can be separated by large distances. The wind does not blow inside the jungle canopy. Flowering plants are the most common rainforest plants. 3. False. 4. Birds, insects and mammals can all be <u>pollinators</u>. <u>Angiosperms</u> is another name for flowering plants.

34 Excel Comprehension Skillbuilder Year 5

Understanding Questions — KID$ With Working Idea$

by Hazel Edwards

Read these reports by children working for money.

Business: Collecting and selling yabbies
Name: Luke
Age: 13
How It works: With a friend, Matthew (13), Luke uses three net tops and about twenty lines in different dams. They go after school and during weekends. Their best catch was 189 yabbies in 35 minutes. Their worst catch was 12 in 3 hours.

On average, they make $15.00–$20.00, charging about $1.10 for a dozen yabbies. Already they have two regular clients.
Problems: It's only a summer business.
Good Things: 'We have lots of fun,' says Luke.

Business: Delivering the local newspapers
Name: Troy
Age: 11
How It Works: On Wednesday nights, the truck drops four big bundles of papers. Troy must deliver them before Thursday night. He makes sure the papers are put in letter boxes so they don't get wet.
Problems: 'I had to fix a new light on my bike,' says Troy. 'Often I don't finish until after dark. The milk crate, which holds the newspapers, came off.'
Good Things: 'My round is close to home,' explains Troy. 'I like riding my bike around the streets. And each week I get $8.25 paid into my bank account.'

1. These words go with Luke or Troy. Can you put them in the right box?(Search and find)

dams	papers	letter boxes	night	yabbies
milk crate	summer	lines	weekends	nets	bike

Luke   **Troy**

_____   _____

_____   _____

_____   _____

_____   _____

_____   _____

_____   _____

Write **short answers** (one or two words) for questions 1 to 3.

1. Who works on Thursdays? _____

2. How much for a dozen yabbies? About $ _____

3. When do Matthew and Luke go yabby catching? _____

4. Draw a line to **match** these sentence beginnings with their right endings.

Troy likes   of papers on Wednesday nights.

Trucks drop big bundles   riding his bike around the streets.

Matthew and Luke go yabbying   after school and on weekends.

5. Troy and Luke could be described as being (lazy   helpful   energetic). (Circle one word.)

6. In **your opinion** who has the best job? _____ because _____

Understanding Questions **35**

Understanding Questions

In cloze exercises you have to select the best word to fill (**close**) the space. To do cloze exercises well you should read the title of the extract, the whole extract and look at any pictures. When you have completed the exercise, read it through again, from the beginning, to make sure it makes good sense.

Read these extracts and answer the questions. (Circle the correct letter — don't write in the space.)

That Proverbial Cat
by Elizabeth Best

Tiger's paws were so sore for the next three days that he willingly stayed around the house. Darin __(1)__ with him. He was full of guilt. Once again his __(2)__ to protect his cat had caused him injury.

Early one morning, when Tiger's sore paws were less tender to __(3)__ on he made a tour of the garden, and when Darin turned his head for a moment, managed to disappear completely.

1. (A) stayed	2. (A) money	3. (A) rest
(B) went	(B) efforts	(B) scratch
(C) tried	(C) dreams	(C) sit
(D) rested	(D) tricks	(D) walk

Own up!
by Ellen Robinson

Dinner was cooking on the stove. It was a gas __(4)__ , so there were always plenty of matches around. The stew was bubbling away fiercely. What if the matchbox fell into the __(5)__? Dreadful thought. Susie quickly reached up to grab the matchbox.

Her hand __(6)__ it when her mother suddenly came in from the yard and banged the door.

4. (A) stove	5. (A) bin	6. (A) smashed
(B) heater	(B) stew	(B) warmed
(C) alarm	(C) hole	(C) touched
(D) pipe	(D) water	(D) emptied

This time you can write the answers on the lines in the spaces.

Going Fishing with my Dad
by Jan Weeks

Dad stood with his oar upright in the river, and was surprised to discover how (7) _____ the water was. Only about waist deep. We could (8) _____ the boat downstream.

I didn't mind. It was like we were having our own (9) _____.

'You know something, Dad?' I said paddling, beside him. 'Fishing's the greatest fun.'

7. (A) cold	8. (A) carry	9. (A) party
(B) muddy	(B) sail	(B) dream
(C) exciting	(C) push	(C) boat
(D) shallow	(D) load	(D) adventure

Understanding Questions

Read the passage and try the **multiple choice questions**. Circle the correct letter.

Sport in the Making — Tennis
by Shane Power

History of the game

The game of tennis played today is a form of the ancient game known as 'royal' tennis. Royal tennis was played on a court with a net. The court could be inside or outside. There are different stories about its origins. One suggestion is that royal tennis goes back to the very early days of Homer, a famous Greek poet. He wrote about a ball game played by a king's daughter and her servants. Another story is that when the knights returned from the crusades in the Middle East around the twelfth century, they introduced the game of tennis to Europe.

However, we do know that in France a game was played with a ball and the palm of the hand. The ball was hit over a net. After a while the player's hands would blister, so gloves were worn to protect the hand.

Players discovered that the glove gave the ball more power.

The next development was strings stretched across the glove. This made the ball travel even faster than before. Finally a bat with a short handle was used by the players. It was called a racquet. The ball was made of leather and was stuffed with hair or cloth.

The French word used to begin the game was *tenez!* It means 'hold' or 'play'. Players would call out this word before they served the ball. It seems that *tenez* became 'tennis' in English.

The English and the French used to enjoy competitions against each other. People from each country began to bet money on the players and the betting became such a big business that tennis was banned.

1. According to the extract the first games of tennis might have been played

   (A) indoors as well as outdoor.

   (B) with a gloved hand.

   (C) with a short handled bat.

   (D) against a wall.

2. The English word **tennis** came to England from

   (A) Greece.

   (B) the Middle East.

   (C) France.

   (D) the Crusades.

3. At one time tennis was banned because

   (A) it caused players to get blisters.

   (B) servants began playing with the princess.

   (C) the ball travelled too quickly.

   (D) people began betting on it.

4. Write the numbers 1 to 4 in the boxes to show the **sequence** in which things occurred.

   ☐ Players used a short handled bat.

   ☐ Tennis was played in England.

   ☐ A glove was used to hit the ball.

   ☐ Strings were stretched across the glove.

Understanding Paragraphs — Introduction

We had an early look at paragraphs in **Finding the Main Idea**. Read page 7 again.

Paragraphs indicate the introduction of new circumstances or people into the writing.

New paragraphs usually show the introduction of:
a change of ideas or characters
a change of place/setting
a change of time
a change of action (what's happening)
a change of speakers in conversation

Each new paragraph starts on a new line. In some writing it is **indented** (about 1cm in).

Paragraphs usually contain:
a topic sentence (see **Finding the Main Idea**)
other sentences providing supporting detail
two to ten sentences

Single sentence paragraphs are used for effect (impact) or in speech/conversations.

Now read the passage *Own Up!* by Ellen Robertson

The children were angry.

One boy at the back of the room banged the desk with his fist. Mrs Lovejoy had specifically promised him a science fiction book.

'Silence!' thundered Mrs McSnorty.

Steve and Suzie were deep in thought. Strangely, they were both remembering a story Mrs Lovejoy had read to them at the beginning of the year. It was about using the power of thought to change things. In fact, the children in the story had even used their power to shrink someone.

But what had their special words been? Finally, Suzie remembered. She whispered to her partner, 'Everyone think *Shrink, Stinker!* — pass it on.'

Then it ran around the room like a miniature railway: *Shrink, Stinker! Shrink, Stinker! Shrink, Stinker!*

Within minutes, all shuffling and fidgeting had stopped. The children sat, hands neatly folded on their desks, staring intently at their teacher.

Just then, the principal poked her head in. It appeared there was no problem after all. Obviously, Mrs Lovejoy had been exaggerating again. What could one expect? She had such a vivid imagination. The principal walked on.

Mrs McSnorty became suspicious. She was peering at the children over her wire-rimmed glasses, when suddenly she discovered that she could only just see over the top of the desk. It towered above her, like Everest.

---

1. Write the number of sentences in each paragraph.

a) Paragraph 2 _____   b) Paragraph 3 _____   c) Paragraph 4 _____

d) Paragraph 5 _____   e) Paragraph 6 _____   f) Paragraph 7 _____

2. What words in para. 8 tell the reader there is a small change in time? _____

3. Why is paragraph 1 just one sentence? (Tick one) ☐ an important event is happening

☐ anger is hard to explain   ☐ someone is speaking   ☐ the story is getting exciting

4. The main person in paragraph 9 is (**the principal**   **the children**   **Mrs McSnorty**).

Answers   1 a. 2, b. 1, c. 4, d. 3, e. 1, f. 2; 2. Just then, 3. an important event is happening, 4. Mrs McSnorty

Understanding Paragraphs — 2

On this page you have four exercises in which you have to select where the paragraph breaks should be. The extracts have been copied without the breaks in place. Slashes have been inserted at the end of sentences. Use a coloured pencil or highlighter to colour the slash where one paragraph ends and a new paragraph begins.

Highlight two places in the extract where new paragraphs should begin. (The first one has been done (with a double slash — //) to help you).

The Incredible Experience of Megan Kingsley by Pamela O'Connor

It was a fine, hot January night. / The light breeze could hardly be felt and caused only faint stirrings in the trees every now and then. // Aurora was already at the cubby house, shaking her head in amusement as Megan and Patrick, loaded down with food, sleeping bags and assorted paraphernalia, staggered down the path. / Aurora, as usual, had brought nothing with her. / Later, they laid out the sleeping bags and placed the food and other things in the corner of the room where Patrick was going to sleep. / He objected loudly but Megan pointed out that as he was the smallest person in there, the least he could do was to make way for a few small items.

In this extract from **The Sylvia Mystery** by Penny Hall, highlight three places where new paragraphs should start.

The next morning, right on time, Kat was up the ladder propped against the back fence. / She peered through the trees but there was nothing to be seen. / She made herself as comfortable as she could and prepared to wait./ From above her head there came a little, breathy giggle, and a voice whispered, 'I'm up here.' / Kat peered up the densely leafed branches overhead. / 'Where? I can't see you.'

In this extract from **Legends of our Land** by Oodgeroo Noonuccal, highlight three places where new paragraphs should start.

Before the whites came, the Noonuccal tribe roamed free over their territory, going on walkabouts, continually on the move, searching for food. / One day they decided to go to the northernmost part of the island, which they called Minjerribah. / Now there was an old woman of the tribe who was always complaining. / This day she was nagging the tribe about food, that she never got enough or it was poor quality and that the tribe treated her badly all the time. / The tribal elders got very angry with her and told her to stop complaining but she would not. / Finally the elders ordered her to be tied to a stake in the ground at the far end of the island. / They told her they would return with food and left her, still growling.

In this extract from **Going fishing with my Dad** by Jan Weeks, highlight five places where new paragraphs should start.

'Caught anything?' Dad asked. / One of them held up a couple of fish as long as my arm./ Dad's eyes almost popped out. / Flathead! / And in the bottom of their boat they had at least a dozen more, all about the same size. They had been caught upriver. / 'You having any luck here?' they asked. / Dad shook his head but couldn't resist telling them about the one that got away, only this time it weighed four kilos, possibly five. / 'It was probably a whale!' I said, loudly enough for Dad to hear.

Relevant and Irrelevant Information **39**

Relevant and Irrelevant Information — Introduction

First we must understand what is meant by the words **relevant** and **irrelevant**.

If something is **relevant** you could also say it is appropriate or of some importance. It has some significance. If it is **irrelevant** then it is the opposite. It is inappropriate, unimportant or insignificant. When writing, only include material relevant to the topic.

It is essential to understand the relevance of information when doing research at school. It is important to know what information to include and what to leave out when we undertake certain tasks or activities. When we write fiction (creative writing) it is important to recognise whether the information is relevant, or not, to our story.

Can you find the irrelevant piece of information in these directions?

How to run a warm bath.
- Put the plug in the plug hole.
- Turn on the hot and cold taps.
- Control the water temperature by adjusting either the hot or cold tap.
- Test the water's temperature by carefully putting your hand in the bath water.
- Make sure the soap is handy.
- Fill the bath to a depth of about 25 cm.

Q. Which point has nothing to do with running a warm bath?

A. Make sure the soap is handy.

Making sure the soap is handy doesn't help to get a bath ready. (It may help you to get clean once you are in the bath!)

Read **Tell me How** by Mike Callaghan, Peter Knapp, Ross Latham and Peter Sloan

---

HOW DO ANTS LIVE?

Ants are social insects that live in large groups called colonies. There are more than 10 000 kinds of ants and they are more numerous than any other land animal. All ants in the colony have special jobs and social responsibilities. Colonies of ants live in well-organised places called nests.

There are three types of ants in a colony: a queen, the female workers and the male ants. The queen ant produces eggs which are cared for by the female worker ants. The male ants are only produced for mating. Most of the ants in a colony are female worker ants.

How a new colony is started

Male ants and new queen ants have wings and are produced in the summer months by the queen of an established colony. When the weather is warm enough they leave the nests for the wedding flight where they mate while flying. After they have mated the male ant falls to the ground and dies. The queen then flies down to the ground and soon after sheds her wings. Once on the ground the queen begins building a new nest.

---

1. If you had to get information on how a new ant colony is started, which of the following facts would be **irrelevant**?

☐ The new queen builds the new nest. ☐ Male ants and new queen ants have wings.

☐ Ants are more numerous than any other animal. ☐ In warm weather ants leave the nest for the wedding flight.

2. Select the most relevant information to complete this sentence. (circle one answer)

To understand ants we must first understand that

(they are social animals   the queen lays eggs   male ants have wings).

Answers   1. Ants are more numerous than any other animal. 2. they are social animals

Relevant and Irrelevant Information — Not Zackly

by Mary Small

Next day, all the rain clouds had disappeared. The sun shone brightly from a clear blue sky.

The gang had assembled in the street to play cricket. Zachary, as usual, hovered in the background. Leigh looked at him. 'We've got to let him play,' he said to Dean.

Dean was astonished. 'Why?' he said.

'Why not?' said Leigh. 'Zachary,' he called. 'Come here.'

Hesitantly, Zachary came towards the group.

'Could you catch a ball?' said Leigh. Zachary looked at the shiny red leather ball that Leigh placed in his hands. He looked at Julie standing waiting, then at all the others. Slowly, he nodded.

'Catch this,' said Leigh and he tossed the ball lightly back to him. It dropped to the ground.

'Zackly's daft,' muttered Brian. 'He can't catch for toffee!'

'His name's Zachary,' said Leigh. 'And he'll learn — you'll see. Just give him practice and time. He can wicket-keep with me.' And that's exactly what Zachary did, not only for that day but for many days after, until he was good enough to try bowling a ball, using a bat and wicket-keeping all on his own.

The gang cheered loudly on the day Zachary scored his first run. He swelled with pride. It was just like Christmas to be a member of the team.

1. Certain information is relevant if we have to describe the type of person Zachary (Zackly) is. Tick the boxes that are relevant to Zachary.

☐ Being allowed to join in helps people to feel accepted for what they are.

☐ Nicknames can make people feel rejected.

☐ To improve cricket skills, it is important to practise.

☐ It was a sunny day for a game of cricket.

2. What words would be irrelevant when applied to Leigh? (tick as many boxes as you need)

☐ caring ☐ lazy ☐ considerate ☐ keen ☐ unsporting ☐ quarrelsome

3. What words would be relevant when applied to Brian? (tick as many boxes as you need)

☐ bossy ☐ selfish ☐ considerate ☐ helpful ☐ friendly ☐ offensive

4. In the extract, what is the most important thing that happens to Zachary? _____

_____

5. What is the most important thing Zachary **does**? (tick one box)

☐ Zachary shares wicket keeping with Leigh. ☐ Zachary scores one run in cricket.

☐ Zachary drops the ball. ☐ Zachary hovered in the background.

Relevant and Irrelevant Information — Show Off

by Hazel Edwards

We went straight past the fairy floss, the Army display (with real guns) and the giant hot air balloon, which they were filling with spurts of gas.

'There's the art and craft hall,' said Matthew, as if he'd just noticed it.

Inside, there were rows of flowers on display. Big glass cases held plates of cakes, each with a label.

'Look at this football,' pointed Matthew.

'That's a cake decorated to look like a football,' said Amanda. She was determined to find her cake. 'Get out of the way, Matt.'

There was a row of fruit cakes.

There was a row of Swiss rolls, with jam oozing from the coils of cake.

And there was a row of patty cakes, with six on each plate.

'Hey. Look at this! A bite. They must have mice in this shed.'

Don't you know *anything*, Matthew? That's where the judges taste to see which one is best.' Amanda was peering anxiously around the glass cases.

'The carrot cakes are down the end. Hundreds of them,' Matthew commented, trying to make Amanda feel better about not getting a prize. He had already checked the name under the First Prize ribbon, curled around the plate. It wasn't Amanda's name.

1. If you were asked to describe the children's search for the carrot cakes what information is relevant in their search? (tick one box)

☐ There was jam oozing out of the Swiss rolls.

☐ The children passed rows of different cakes.

☐ Real guns were used in the Army display.

☐ Matthew thought there were mice in the shed.

2. What words would be irrelevant when applied to Matthew? (tick as many boxes as you need)

☐ protective ☐ spiteful ☐ considerate ☐ keen ☐ supportive ☐ selfish

3. What words would be relevant when applied to Amanda? (tick as many boxes as you need)

☐ embarrassed ☐ proud ☐ determined ☐ helpful ☐ frightened ☐ anxious

4. From the extract, what is the most important thing that Matthew knows? _____

_____

5. It is important that Matthew finds the carrot cakes first. True ☐ False ☐

6. The cakes were in the art and craft hall. True ☐ False ☐

7. There were at least three children in the group. True ☐ False ☐

Relevant and Irrelevant Information — Paddock for a Pony

by Elizabeth Best

School was out. The bell had rung and the children erupted from every doorway — some to go running wildly towards their homes as if their lives depended upon it, some to line up to catch buses under the watchful eye of their teacher, and many more to walk off in groups or pairs in any one of several directions.

Deborah was with her best friend, Pat. They were in a hurry but today they did not run, only walked quickly, hardly speaking at all, intent on getting to Pat's place. At the weekend one of Pat's guinea pigs had had four babies, and Deborah was to see them for the first time.

Half a kilometre from school, they arrived. Opening the gate, running now, they flung their school bags onto the lawn and flew around the back.

Firstly, the dog had to be locked away. Then, when enticing with grass failed to make the babies appear, the lid of the darkened nest had to be opened. At last, Deborah held one of the tiny animals right in her hands.

She was enraptured. The darling little thing! She sat down on the grass, holding it gently, taking care not to squeeze it or hurt it in any way. It was perfect, so exactly like its mother, with its soft fur and little twitching nose — only in miniature. It sat up in her hands and rubbed two tiny paws over its nose as if it had just been taught.

'You can only hold it for a minute,' Pat said importantly. 'For a few minutes, anyway. Otherwise its mother might go off it.'

1. What information is **relevant** when understanding the excitement Pat and Deborah share? (tick as many boxes as you need)

☐ Pat and Deborah had finished school for the day.

☐ Pat and Deborah walked home in silence.

☐ Pat and Deborah threw their bags onto the lawn.

☐ Pat and Deborah locked the dog away.

2. What is the cause of Pat and Deborah's excitement? _____

_____

3. What words would be **irrelevant** when applied to Pat? (tick as many boxes as you need)

☐ proud ☐ stubborn ☐ friendly ☐ upset ☐ angry ☐ rough

4. What words would be relevant when applied to Deborah? (tick as many boxes as you need)

☐ bossy ☐ conceited ☐ shy ☐ excited ☐ happy ☐ dreamy

5. For Deborah, what is the most important thing she does? (circle one letter)

(A) She finishes school for the day.
(B) She walks home with Pat.
(C) She feeds the guinea pigs grass.
(D) She holds a baby guinea pig in her hands.

Fact and Opinion — Introduction

Facts and opinions are part of our everyday speech and writing. It is important to recognise when someone is trying to persuade you to do or believe something (See Understanding Persuasion, p. 47).

A fact is something that everyone agrees with and can usually be proved either by direct observation or clear written records.

An opinion is a particular viewpoint of the writer or speaker.

An opinion often:
- is personal,
- is used to influence (or convince) the reader or listener,
- provides suggestions on courses of action.

Read this short passage from *Not Another Ad!* by John D. Fitzgerald.

Films (on TV) are interrupted by advertisements about every eleven minutes. 　Many ads we see on television are boring, or just plain silly. Advertisements for	one brand of car that show two men beating each other over the head tell us nothing about the car they are trying to sell.

Fact: *Films are interrupted by advertisements about every eleven minutes*. We could easily prove this by doing a count of ads during a TV film.

Opinion: *Many ads we see on television are boring*. They might be boring for many people but there could be those viewers who are entertained, amused or informed by what they see.

Opinion: *(Many ads are) just plain silly*. The same comments, as above, apply.

Fact: *two men beating each other over the head tell us nothing about the car*. This could be checked by watching the ad.

Try this extract from an interview.

Radio Current Affairs
by Elizabeth Halley

Elizabeth Halley:　Has television taken over from radio? Paul Murphy:　　Radio is making a comeback; for instance 'PM' (a radio news show) has increased its audience by 160% over the past two years, and these are national figures. I compete against commercial radio for a start, but also against commercial television. There will always be an enormous future for radio in Australia because it's portable. Although television is getting a bit that way, it's not quite so portable. You can't watch television while you drive your car.

Write **fact** or **opinion** after these short extracts from the interview

1. '**PM**' (a radio news show) has increased its audience by 160%. _____

2. There will always be an enormous future for radio in Australia. _____

3. Radio is making a comeback. _____

4. Television is not quite so portable (as radio)._____

Answers　1. fact, 2. opinion, 3. fact, 4. fact

Fact and Opinion — 2

Read the extracts on this page and answer the questions on **fact and opinion**.

Battlers of the Great Depression

by Edel Wignell

(During the Great Depression) life was difficult for the women at home. Most people did not own vacuum cleaners, washing machines or any other modern equipment, so housework was drudgery. Many households had only one tap, which might be in the backyard, so people carried water in buckets and heated it in kettles. Imagine how much water was carried for washing dishes and clothes, and baths for a family of six!

1. Tick the box that is an **opinion** which is taken from the extract.

☐ Most people did not own vacuum cleaners. ☐ Housework was drudgery.

☐ Many households had only one tap. ☐ People carried water in buckets.

2. As you have read, (Fact and Opinion — Introduction), opinions try to influence the reader. The reader is meant to react to the above extract by

☐ giving money to the poor. ☐ understanding the difficulties of the time.

☐ helping with housework at home. ☐ making sure all houses have enough taps.

Made for Australia

by Judith Kendra

Before the Second World War it is fair to say that there was not very much good scientific work going on in Australia. However, things changed completely after the war. Brilliant scientists came to Australia — mostly from Britain and Europe.

In the aircraft world, David Warren came up with the idea for the black box flight recorder. This has since been a great saver of lives. Another invention, Interscan, is an Australian aircraft landing system designed by Dr Paul Wild and his CSIRO team. In 1965, Qantas invented an award-winning escape raft, called a slide raft. This is now used in many aeroplanes throughout the world if they have to land on water.

1. Tick the boxes that are **facts** taken from the above extract.

☐ There was not much good scientific work going on in Australia.

☐ Scientists came to Australia from Britain and Europe.

☐ Things changed completely after the war.

☐ The slide raft was invented by Qantas.

2. Which phrase warns the reader that the information is an opinion? (tick one box)

☐ it is fair to say ☐ designed by Dr Paul Wild ☐ in the aircraft world

3. It is a **fact** that many aeroplanes use the slide raft invention. True ☐ False ☐

Fact and Opinion — Not Another Ad!

by John D. Fitzgerald

Letterbox rubbish overload

Many people complain about the quantity of advertising material left in their letterboxes every week. Brochures, catalogues, leaflets for new shops and seasonal sales, hand delivered letters from real estate agents looking for houses to buy or sell, and other material are left. Some of the letterboxes have signs on them asking that 'no junk mail' be left, but it does not seem to stop the deliveries.

This unwanted material can often be seen blowing around the streets, lying in gutters, or strewn over lawns. As well as adding to the amount of paper used it also litters the neighbourhood.

Another problem with this form of advertising is that it lets people know when there is no one at home and provides a perfect invitation for thieves. When we are going away we can cancel deliveries of milk and newspapers, but there seems to be no way of cancelling the advertising material. A letterbox overflowing with advertisements is a sure sign to housebreakers that nobody's home.

1. Tick the boxes that are **facts** taken from the extract.

   ☐ The unwanted material can often be seen blowing around the streets.

   ☐ Uncollected milk bottles provide a perfect invitation for thieves.

   ☐ When we are going away we can cancel deliveries of newspapers.

   ☐ Many people complain about advertising material left in their letterboxes.

2. 'A letterbox overflowing with advertisements is a sure sign to housebreakers that nobody's home.' This information is an opinion. True ☐ False ☐

3. It is a **fact** that junk mail can be seen blowing around the street. True ☐ False ☐

4. Many people get advertising material in their letterboxes. Tick the boxes to show the material your family has received.

   ☐ brochures   ☐ real estate material   ☐ shop sales advertising

   ☐ catalogues   ☐ cafe/restaurant advertising

5. How could you find out whether or not people wanted letterbox advertising material?

   _____

6. Can you think of a reason (other than the one in the extract) why a letterbox might be overflowing with advertising material? (short answer) _____

7. Where might you get information to prove that overflowing letterboxes 'provide an invitation to thieves'?(short answer) _____

8. Generally, the writer's opinion is that junk mail is of little value. True ☐ False ☐

46 Excel Comprehension Skillbuilder Year 5

Fact and Opinion — My Diary

by Jenny Jarman-Walker

Note: Although this is a fictional diary it is a good place to look at fact and opinion. It is a 'realistic' piece of writing.

Monday 10th April

Dear Diary,

I'm writing in the taxi on the way to the TV studio. It's 6.45 in the morning and it's just getting light. It was dark and cold when my alarm went off, and I wanted to stay in bed a bit longer. Mum said, 'No.'

Mr Davis is driving me this morning. He doesn't talk much, which is good. I can write more. I can see the grass on the side of the road. It's still wet. It's supposed to be sunny later on. Let's hope so. I hate it when filming stops because of the rain.

My 'call' is for 7.30. Before we finish work every day we are all given a call sheet. It has all the information about what we'll be doing the next day, which scenes we'll be filming (or 'shooting' as they say), and what time

everyone has to be at work. Under my name is 'Call time 7.30 am.', and, 'Scenes 4, 5 and 7'.

Hey, we're here already. I'll run out of the taxi as fast as I can and into the studio so I can stay warm.

It's 8.00 and I have changed into my wardrobe for today. I know 'wardrobe' sounds funny, as if I should have knobs or handles, but that's what they call what I'm wearing today.

I have three scenes to shoot before lunch today. I know my lines. Mum helped me last night.

Mandy, the make-up and hair-dressing lady, is pulling my hair into a ponytail, so it's hard to write. She's done my make-up already. Yuk! I hate this stuff. How does Mum put up with it all day?

1. Tick the box that is an opinion taken from the extract.

☐ It was dark and cold when my alarm went off.

☐ It's 8.00 and I have changed into my wardrobe for today.

☐ Mr Davis doesn't talk much, which is good.

☐ I have three scenes to shoot before lunch today.

2. This writing comes from a _____ which should prepare the reader for writing that contains facts as well as _____.

Answer the next 3 questions with information according to the extract.

3. It is a **fact** that it was dark and cold when the alarm went off.　True ☐　False ☐

4. The writer is expressing a **fact**, then an **opinion**, when she writes 'I have changed into my wardrobe for today. I know 'wardrobe' sounds funny.'　True ☐　False ☐

5. The writer states that she wanted to stay in bed a bit longer. This is an opinion.　True ☐　False ☐

6. 'Mum helped me last night.' This is (a fact　an opinion). (circle one answer)

7. It is a fact that the diary writer ☐ is looking for work. ☐ is about to start work. (tick one)

Understanding Persuasion — Introduction

Almost without being aware of it, we are bombarded with persuasion everyday. You cannot watch television, listen to the radio or read a magazine without advertisements. Advertisements are trying to get you to choose a particular **product** or **service**. In fact, you can't drive down the road with seeing advertisements.

But there are other ways people use persuasion. Your friends at school may try to persuade you to join them in a game. Another student may try to persuade you that he or she is the best person for class or school captain. These people are trying to persuade you to think in a particular way.

They are trying to influence your **thinking**.

Persuasive writing has some special features.
- It tries to attract the reader's attention.
- It may use a mixture of **logical** and **emotive** language.
- It sounds **convincing** (as if the writer is an expert!).
- It may contain a **slogan** and a **concluding statement**.
- It often appears to address the reader/listener in a personal way.
Read this ad from a tourist magazine.

Let the world know you're having a
Great Holiday
No matter where you are!

Rent a Tropical Islands Mobile Phone
UNITING PEOPLE ACROSS OCEANS
Also available: phonecards, faxes, business phones

Learning Points
The ad:
- speaks to the reader directly by using the words 'you' and 'you're'
- attracts the reader's attention by a picture and big print for the heading
- appeals to your emotions more than your common sense (logic)
- gives the impression that this could be happening for you right now!
- lets 'you' see yourself lazing under a palm tree, ringing 'your' friends
- makes use of a slogan
- uses a concluding statement (other products available for rent)

1. Who are you supposed to think of instead of the person under the tree? _____

2. What is the slogan for the rental company? _____

3. This ad appeals to your common sense.   True ☐   False ☐

Short Answers
1. yourself, 2. Uniting People Across Oceans, 3. False

Understanding Persuasion — What a Waste!

by Stephen Jones

In his book *What a Waste!*, Stephen Jones tries to persuade the reader to be a more active protector of the environment. Read this extract and answer the questions, remembering the things you have read about persuasion.

SOLVING PROBLEMS IN THE FUTURE
Writing to politicians
Politicians are elected to govern the country according to the wishes of the people. You can help get politicians to pass laws protecting the environment by writing to them or by joining groups that lobby them.

Cradle to grave design
In the past, designers were only concerned about how well the products they designed worked. They did not worry about what happened to them after they were thrown away. People are now starting to demand products that do not harm the environment, especially as the cost of disposing waste rises. Designers will, in the future, have to consider the effects on the environment of disposing of their product. This is called cradle to the grave design.

Imagination
The most important resource of all that we have to help us solve the problems of a throwaway society is our imagination. All of us need to use our imagination to think of new ways of solving the problems of waste. Our imagination is one resource that will never be used up. Not to make use of it would be the worst waste of all.

Writing letters is one way of drawing attention to a problem you think should be fixed. Some people write to newspapers (letters to the editor), some people write letters of complaint to organisations, trying to persuade them to change the way they act.

1. To whom should people write to get good environmental laws? _____

2. What words does the writer use to make you think that you should be involved in saving the environment? (tick the boxes)

   ☐ you ☐ waste ☐ designers ☐ imagination ☐ us ☐ grave

3. This extract is meant to make you feel (tick the boxes)

   ☐ sad ☐ helpless ☐ hopeful ☐ imaginative ☐ motivated

4. Which one of these sentences sums up what the extract is telling us? (tick one box)

   ☐ Not to make use of your imagination would be the worst waste of all.

   ☐ People are starting to demand products that do not harm the environment.

   ☐ Designers will have to consider the effects of disposing of their products.

   ☐ Politicians are elected to govern the country.

5. How does the writer arouse the reader's interest? (tick one box)

   ☐ He makes his writing amusing.

   ☐ He uses a heading that makes the reader think the article is important.

   ☐ He selects subjects that are unusual.

   ☐ He uses short paragraphs so that the information is easy to read.

Understanding Persuasion — Saving Wildlife

by Edel Wignel

Save the habitat

The best way to save wildlife is to save their habitat (the places where they live).

People are the greatest threat to wildlife. People cause pollution by throwing rubbish, riding trail bikes through the bush, and stirring up mud in streams with outboard motors.

Logging the forest destroys the habitat of many animals. When people cut down forests for timber, mining or farming, the wildlife vanishes. People try to restore the habitat, but this is impossible. The area will never be the same again. Some places can be partly restored but they will be different from the original habitat.

For many years, people have been working to save the forest wildernesses of south eastern Tasmania, and rainforest, such as the Daintree, in northern Queensland. Destruction of rainforests means death for hundreds of species of flora and fauna.

For example, there are only three species of cassowary in the world. One is the southern cassowary which lives in the rainforests of northern Queensland. It is a flightless bird, two metres tall. Cassowaries feed on fungi and fruit which falls from rainforest trees and vines. They cannot be kept in captivity.

1. The writer uses some words and phrases that appeal to the reader's emotions. Other information adds to the reader's understanding. Tick the boxes for the statements that contain **emotive** language.

   ☐ Destruction of rainforests means death for many species of fauna.

   ☐ People try to restore the habitat, but this is impossible.

   ☐ The best way to save wildlife is to save their habitat.

   ☐ There are only three species of cassowary in the world.

2. The extract is meant to make the reader feel that there is a problem which (tick one box)

   ☐ needs everyone's attention.　　☐ governments should do something about.

   ☐ will soon be solved.　　☐ has no solution.

3. This extract is meant to make you feel (tick the boxes)

   ☐ angry　☐ helpful　☐ hopeless　☐ informed　☐ motivated

4. The heading is used to (tick one box)

   ☐ arouse the reader's attention.　　☐ inform the reader about the author.

   ☐ provide answers to important questions.　　☐ encourage people to plant trees.

5. The writer provides factual information to support her concern.　True ☐　False ☐

6. The writer opens the extract by stating her beliefs.　True ☐　False ☐

7. The writer uses humour to hold the reader's interest.　True ☐　False ☐

50 Excel Comprehension Skillbuilder Year 5

Understanding Persuasion — Going Fishing With My Dad

by Jan Weeks

Now for something different! This is not a factual passage but it illustrates how the narrator tries to persuade his father to take him fishing. As you read (see Context Clues p. 17) the extract, think of the strategies the narrator uses.

Remember: The person who tells the story/poem is often called the **narrator** if we don't know his/her name.

'Fishing is the greatest fun,' said my father. Mum had asked him to mow the back lawn, but the mower wouldn't start so he was leaning over the back fence talking to our neighbours instead. They'd spent the weekend fishing and had come back with stacks of fish. We even had some in our refrigerator.

I thought fishing would be the greatest fun as well, so I jumped up and down and begged Dad to take me. Asking for something in front of neighbours was always a good idea. No father wanted to look mean in front of his neighbours. 'Sure, son,' he answered, patting my head.

'When?' I asked, trying to pin him to a definite date. All he said was 'One of these days,' which probably meant never.

During the next week I weeded the garden and pestered Dad to take me fishing. I washed the car and pestered Dad to take me fishing. I tidied the garage and pestered Dad to take me fishing.

'All right,' he said at last, worn down by my persistence.

1. The narrator uses a number of schemes to get his father to agree to take him fishing. These include (tick the boxes)

☐ embarrassing his father.

☐ getting his own fishing gear.

☐ pestering his father.

☐ being helpful around the house.

2. What did Dad do to avoid saying yes to the narrator's pleas?(tick one box)

☐ gave his son lots of work to do.

☐ agreed, without giving a definite time to go.

☐ ignored his son's pleading.

☐ gave good reasons why he couldn't take his son with him.

3. Dad agreed to take his son fishing because it was a good idea.   True ☐   False ☐

4. Dad agreed to take his son fishing as a reward for hard work.   True ☐   False ☐

5. Do you think the narrator would have kept pestering if tidying the shed hadn't worked? (give your reason)

6. The narrator's actions probably (tick one box)

☐ amazed the father.

☐ pleased the father.

☐ annoyed the father.

☐ amused the father.

Understanding and Using Tables of Contents — Introduction

Most factual books have Tables of Contents. These are found in the front of the book, usually within the first few pages. Tables of Contents are a quick reference which help readers find the main sections of the book. Some books are broken up into major sections, subjects or topics and within each section or subject area there are sub-sections.

Some fiction books may also have a table of contents. These may give the location of the chapters or, if a book of many works, the place in the book of the individual stories, plays or poems.

Here is a Table of Contents from *Puppets* by Carole Hooper.

usually less than one page

sub-sections

A **glossary** is an alphabetical list of unusual words and their meanings.

List of other books referred to in the text.

page numbers

major subject headings

An **index** gives a quick page reference to less important information.

Contents

Introduction	**5**
A history of puppets	**6**
Types of puppets	**16**
Glove or hand puppets	17
Marionette	18
Rod puppets	21
Shadow puppets	22
Some special puppets from around the world	**24**
Vietnamese water puppets	24
Javanese shadow puppets	24
Southern Indian marionettes	29
Japanese bunraku-za	32
Making puppets	**36**
Papier-mâché puppet	36
Shadow puppets	37
Bibliography	**40**

1. On what page would you find rod puppets? (short answer) page _____

2. Under what heading would you find information about puppets from other countries? (short answer) _____

3. The section, **Types of Puppets**, begins on page 16.   True ☐ False ☐

4. The section, **History of Puppets**, is the longest section.   True ☐ False ☐

5. If you wanted to make a shadow puppet you would turn to page 22. True ☐ False ☐

6. If you wanted to find other books about puppets you would check the _____.

7. The **Introduction** is at the _____ of the book. The **Bibliography** is at the _____.

Answers   1. page 21, 2. Some special puppets from around the world, 3. True, 4. True, 5. True, 6. Bibliography, 7. front, back

Understanding and Using Tables of Contents — What a Waste!

by Stephen Jones

Note: Some books also have an **index** which is an alphabetical list of sub-topics and references to be found in the book. The index will include page numbers.

Contents

Introduction	2
Recycling waste in nature	4
Waste through the ages	8
The throwaway society	15
What we throw away	18
How we dispose of solid waste and liquid waste	25
Difficult wastes	30
Gaseous waste	31
Beyond the throwaway society	37
Understanding packaging	40
Materials that can be recycled	42
Recycling — the benefits, the problems	50
Beyond recycling	52
Solving problems in the future	54
How much do we waste, how much do we recycle?	58
Glossary	60
Index	61
Pronunciation guide	62

1. On what page will you find the index? (short answer) _____

2. On what page will you find information on **gaseous wastes**? (short answer) _____

3. What topic is found on page 58? _____

4. The word **compost** is used in the book. Where would I first look to find all references to **compost** in the book? In the _____.

5. What would you expect to find in the Pronunciation guide? _____
_____

6. Where in the book would you find the **Contents** page? In the _____.

7. The topic, **Recycling waste**, is 4 pages long.   True ☐   False ☐

8. The last three sections are there to help you use the book.   True ☐   False ☐

9. On which page would you find the history of disposing of waste? _____

Understanding and Using an Index — Introduction

Many factual books have indexes. They are found in the back of the book. Indexes are a quick reference which help readers find the information in a book that is not easily found using the Table of Contents. The index items are listed **alphabetically** and give one, or more pages, where information may be found. References longer than one page are shown by using a hyphen (eg 34–37).

One of the main skills in using an index is finding the right reference word. If you wanted to find some information on *motor cars* you might have to look under *cars*. If you wanted to find information on *rainfall* you might have to look under *weather*. If you don't find what you are looking for the first time try some other possibilities.

Indexes may also have their own conventions. The main entry may not be repeated to save space (a bit like a dictionary). If you wanted to find *radio advertisement* you have to look up *radio* under *advertisements*. It is grouped with other types of advertisements.

Not Another Ad!
by John D. Fitzgerald

Index (incomplete)

advertisements 13, 18-25, 37, 39, 44–45, 73, 79–80
  electronic 13, 14, 47
  entertainment 38
  fashion 13
  jingles 38
  radio 13, 38
  (*see also* newspaper advertisements, outdoor advertisements, printed advertisements, radio advertisements, television advertisements)
advertising 10–12, 25, 36, 46–47, 50, 59, 78–79, 81
  false 25

people ignored by 32
  unwanted 12, 47, 51–54, 74, 81
  advertisers 19, 30–36, 45
clutter 65
comics 19, 46
community announcements 37
emotions 21
environment 65, 69
  recycling 51
  pollution 35
  visual pollution 53, 65, 69
famous people 44
film and television stars 24
hidden messages 26-29, 55
junk mail 51, 53–54, 81

letterboxes 11, 12, 46, 51, 54, 55, 81
magazines 13, 46, 49, 70
newspaper advertisements 11, 12, 13, 46, 48–51, 56-57
  Melbourne *Age* 50
outdoor advertisements 13, 59, 65–66, 69–70
  billboards 13, 59, 63, 65
  bus-stops 13, 59
  buses 13, 63
  landmarks 70
  railway stations 13, 59
  taxis 13, 63
printed advertisements 3, 46–47, 57–58. 79–80

---

1. On what page would you find information on emotions? (short answer) _____

2. How many references are there to *comics* in the **Not Another Ad!** index? (short answer) _____

3. If you wanted to find out about recycling, you would look under _____.

4. There are five different types of *Outdoor Advertising* listed.   True ☐ False ☐

5. In the entry **advertising** the word *false* is short for **false advertising**. True ☐ False ☐

6. The most information on **junk mail** commences on page (**51 53 81**). (circle one answer)

Answers 1. p. 21, 2. 2, 3. environment, 4. False, 5. True, 6. p. 53 (to p. 54)

54 Excel Comprehension Skillbuilder Year 5

Made For Australia

by Judith Kendra

This (incomplete) index looks a little different to the index in **Not Another Ad!** It is important that we get used to the number of different ways indexes may be organised.

INDEX

Aeronautical Research		Balmain bug	20	Chaffey, George and William	29
Laboratories	38	Bandt, Lewis	27	Chanel	15
A Town Like Alice	24	Bathurst Island	17	Charlton, Andrew 'Boy'	44
Acton, Prue	14	Beaurepaire, Frank	44	cheese	18
AIDS	30	Bionic ear	34–35	Clarke, Professor Graeme	35
Akubra hat	19, 24	black box recorder	37, 38	Commodore	13
Alston, James	28	Blackmores Laboratories	8	Commonwealth Games	45
Andrews, Gordon	14	Bondi Surf Bathers Life		Communications	40–41
Angels, The	48	Saving Club	46	Connyngham, Barry	48
Artificial rain	29	Bonynge, Richard	48	Coolgardie Safe	8–9
AUSSAT	40–41	Bosito, Joseph	31	Cracknell, Ruth	48
Aussie Gold	24	Brack, John	47	Culgoora	42
Australian Telescope	42	Bright, William	50	CSIRO	37
Australian Ballet Company	48	Burke and Wills	26	Davis, Jack	48
Australian crawl	44	Cafe bar	42–43	Davis, Judy	48
Australian Inland Mission	52	Carey, Peter	47	Delice de France	18
Australian National University	12	Cavill, Percy and Richard	44	Denver, John	25

---

1. On what page would you find information on Bathurst Island? (short answer) _____

2. How many references are there to *black box recorder*? (short answer) _____

3. The reference on **Bionic ear** commences on page 34 and finishes on page _____.

4. What page do you go to to find information on Peter Carey? _____

5. The entry **Commodore** comes before **Cafe Bar**.   True ☐   False ☐

6. To find the entry to The Angels you have to look under Angels, The. Can you think of a

   reason why? _____

7. **Jack Davis** appears before **Judy Davis** in the index. This is because he is more

   important.   True ☐   False ☐

8. Select the best ending for this sentence beginning. There are

   ☐ two pages of information on **Akubra hats**.

   ☐ references to **Akubra hats** on two different pages.

9. The index in **Made For Australia** is arranged in page number order.

   True ☐   False ☐

Using Timetables — Introduction

Timetables play an important part in our lives. Some of us use timetables for bus or train travel. We have lesson timetables at school but we also have timetables for sports days and swimming carnivals. The program for the school concert is a timetable.

Timetables are a list of events according to time — when things are on. Without timetables we could be late for school or work. We could miss out on things we want to do. Timetables help us to keep our lives in order.

This is the timetable (or program) for a beach carnival.

Sandy Coast Annual Beach Sports Day

Time	Event	Location	Learning points
9.00 am	Half court basketball	South end of beach	am — morning
9.30–12 noon	School bands	Promenade	Continuing events
	Face painting	Pavilion	
	Kite flying display	Picnic Park	
	Radio SCB Give-aways	Pavilion	
10.15 am	Inline skate display	Promenade	
10.45 am	Ocean Drive fun run	Ocean Drive	
11.00 am	Junior Life Saving Competition.	Clubhouse beach front	
12 noon	Surf boat relays	Clubhouse beach front	pm — afternoon
2.00 pm	Ironman Contest	Clubhouse beach front	
2.30 pm	Surfboard rescue display	Clubhouse beach front	
3.00 pm	First aid demonstration	Pavilion	
3.00 pm	Touch football — mixed teams	South end of beach	
3.30 pm	Helicopter rescue display	Clubhouse beach front	
4.00 pm	Beach races (juniors)	North end of beach	
4.30 pm	Presentation of trophies	Clubhouse beach front	Concluding event

Give short answers for questions 1 to 6.

1. When do the surfboat relays start? _____ **2.** The surf boat relays last for __ hours.

3. When could you see the helicopter? _____ **4.** When does the fun run start? _____

5. Where is the kite flying? _____ **6.** Where is face painting? _____

7. Name an event held at the south end of the beach. _____ .

8. You could listen to the school band at 11 am. True ☐ False ☐

9. The helicopter rescue display will most likely last for two hours. True ☐ False ☐

Answers 1. 12 noon, 2. two hours, 3. 3.30 pm, 4. 10.45 am 5. Picnic Park. 6. Pavilion, 7. touch football or basketball, 8. True, 9. False

Using Timetables — Train Timetables

Bus and train timetables often require the reading of tables. You may have to read across the table as well as up and down the table.

Route S 12 — Night Rider

Timetable for Monday to Saturday

TRAIN FROM	pm	pm	pm	TRAIN FROM	pm	pm	am
Town Hall	7.30	9.30	11.30	East Hills	8.10	10.10	12.10
Central	7.40	9.40		Revesby	8.20	10.20	
Newtown	7.50	9.50	11.45	Bankstown	8.35	10.35	12.45
Lakemba	8.25	10.25		Lakemba	8.50	10.50	
Bankstown	8.40	10.40	12.25 am	Newtown	9.25	11.25	1.25
Revesby	8.55	10.55		Central	9.35	11.35	
East Hills	9.05	11.05	12.45 am	Town Hall	9.45	11.45	1.45

Give **short answers** for questions 1 to 8.

1. How many Night Rider trips from Town Hall to East Hills? _____

2. At what time does the 8.10 pm East Hill train arrive at Central? _____

3. This is a timetable for every day except _____ .

4. How many Town Hall trains leave before midnight but arrive at East Hills after

    midnight? _____

5. What East Hills train should you catch if you have to get to Central by 11 pm? _____

6. How long does the 9:30 Town Hall train take to get to Lakemba? _____ minutes.

7. The train that leaves Bankstown at 8.35 pm gets to Newtown at _____.

8. The longest part of the journey is between _____ and _____ .

9. The last train from East Hills does not stop at Central.   True ☐   False ☐

10. The 11:30 pm Town Hall train stops at Bankstown.   True ☐   False ☐

11. If I catch the 8.10 train from East Hills to Bankstown, the first return train I can catch

    leaves at _____.

12. How many Night Rider trains stop at Central? _____

13. Why do you think the 11:30 pm Town Hall train is quicker than the other trains?

Understanding Maps — Introduction

We usually think of **atlases** when we think of maps. But maps can be found in many other places. Most people who live in big cities use a **street directory**. People who do a lot of travelling might use a **road map**. People interested in the universe might use a **star map**. When studying maps we are usually interested in distance, direction and location.

This map comes from *What's Cooking?* by Kerri Bingle, David Bowden and Jenny Dibley (p. 59)

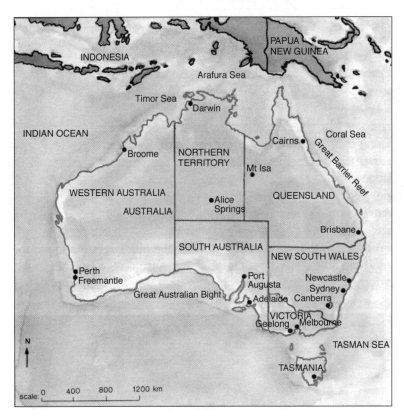

Important Points

Direction: This is shown by the compass point in the lower left corner. Learn all the compass points.

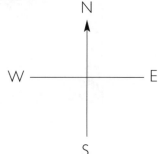

Distance: This can be worked out using the scale line. The distance from Victoria to Tasmania is about 0.5 cm which is about 225 km. (9 mm shows 400 km)

Give **short answers** for questions 1 to 6.

If you were in Alice Springs which direction would you go to get to:-

1. Queensland? _____
2. Arafura Sea? _____
3. Western Australia? _____
4. Great Australian Bight? _____
5. Which sea is north of Broome? _____
6. About how far is it across South Australia? _____ km
7. Australia's closest neighbour is (Papua New Guinea Indonesia Darwin). (circle one)

Answers
1. east, 2. north, 3. west, 4. south, 5. Timor Sea, 6. about 1 100 km. 7. Papua New Guinea

Understanding Maps — What's Cooking (Greece)

by Kerri Bingle, David Bowden and Jenny Dibley (p. 9)

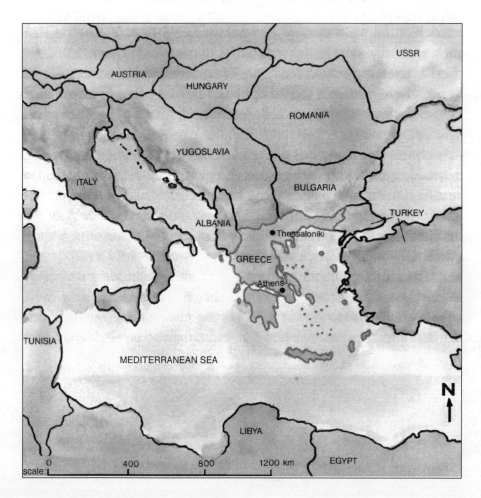

Give **short answers** for questions 1 to 9.

If you were in Athens (Greece) which direction would you go to get to:-

1. Bulgaria _____   2. Libya _____   3. Romania _____

4. Turkey _____   5. Italy _____   6. Tunisia _____

7. Which country is west of Hungary? _____

8. Which countries separate Greece and the USSR? _____

9. Which sea would you have to cross to get from Athens to Egypt? _____

10. The trip from Athens to Egypt is about _____ km.

11. Bulgaria shares a border with Hungary   True ☐ False ☐

12. The maps for Australia (p. 57) and Greece have the same scale. True ☐ False ☐

Understanding Graphs and Charts — Introduction

Graphs and charts provide information that has to be read in a particular way. Charts, graphs and tables (see p. 55) require you to understand how the information is presented, as well as interpreting the information provided.

Charts and graphs are a simple way of providing information without a lot of reading.

In maths you may have learnt that graphs come in many forms. These include pictographs, bar or column graphs, line graphs and pie graphs. Information in many books is often provided in graph form because it can save lengthy explanations. Most graphs show the relationship between two pieces of information.

This **graph** is a type of bar or column graph. It has a single bar which has been broken up into sections to show proportions (percentages). It is made interesting by turning the bar into a wheelie (rubbish) bin.

What a Waste
by Stephen Jones

Household Rubbish

Plastics

5%
5%
5% — Other / Metals
15% — Glass
20% — Garden waste
25% — Paper

Percentages of household waste in Australia
25% — Food scraps

1. All the rubbish in this bin comes from _____.

2. Most household rubbish is either _____ or _____.

3. Car batteries would be included in the section called **Other**. True ☐ False ☐

4. Most household rubbish could be recycled. (You'll have to work it out.) True ☐ False ☐

5. Name one thing you think would be included in **Garden Waste**. _____

6. Does this graph mean that everyone has a full wheelie bin each week? Yes ☐ No ☐

Answers

1. households, 2. paper or food, 3. True, 4. True, 5. grass clippings, (other answers possible), 6. No

Understanding Charts — The Portland Fairy Penguins

The chart below comes from **The Portland Fairy Penguins** by Edel Wignell. It shows the activity of fairy penguins over a period of one year, month by month.

Note: when you first look at this diagram it appears that chick raising happens twice a year; in January and again from September to December. But January follows December. There is really only one chick raising period — September to the next January.

The Penguin Calendar

Give **short answer**s for questions 1 and 2.

1. How many penguin activities are shown on the chart? _____

2. When do chicks begin to hatch each year? _____

3. How many months does **chick raising** last? _____ months

4. **Nest building** happens (before   after) **egg laying**. (circle one word)

5. Egg laying happens for about six months.   True ☐   False ☐

6. Moulting (chicks losing baby feathers) lasts for about three months.   True ☐   False ☐

7. Nest building happens in the month of May.   True ☐   False ☐

8. What activity happens straight after **moulting**? (tick one box)

   ☐ chick raising   ☐ egg laying   ☐ nest building   ☐ burrow attendance

9. The two activities that happen in July are _____ and _____.